VIDEO GOALS: Getting Results With Pictures And Sound
(Revised)

By Tom Schroeppel

LIBRARY OF CONGRESS CATALOG CARD NUMBER 86-91773

ISBN 0-9603718-2-6

6th Printing

For Ernie and Boots Schroeppel,
My parents and my best friends.
I love you.

TABLE OF CONTENTS

Preface

The manuals that come with film and video equipment explain clearly how to operate the tools of our profession. What they don't explain is how to use those tools to make consistently good programs--programs that achieve their goals. That's the purpose of this book.

I make non-fiction, non-theatrical films and videos. In the following pages, I'll show you how I approach my craft. The suggested techniques should work for you, or at least serve as a basis for developing a successful work method of your own.

Some of the information presented in Chapter Five, "Directing and Shooting," is also covered in my book, "The Bare Bones Camera Course For Film And Video," from the point of view of the cameraperson. This overlap, while necessary, is more a reinforcement than a duplication. The two books were designed to complement each other.

Language note: English does not yet have a proper set of pronouns for the abstract third personal singular. Therefore each writer must make [his, her, his/her] own decision as to how [he, she, he/she, h/she] decides to deal with this situation. For clarity, I generally use the traditional masculine form, with the understanding that it represents both genders. So, for example, when I speak of the viewer and his reactions, I'm talking about any viewer, male or female.

1. Sending Messages/Making Chairs

We're all message-senders. We all send messages with pictures and sounds.

It's a natural process. A baby smiles, and sends the message, "I'm happy." He cries, and we know he's sad.

As the baby grows, he learns to send more complex messages: "I hope I can pass my math test on Friday," "Sweetheart, I swear I'll love you till the day I die," "Mr. Johnson, here's an artist's rendering of your new shopping center."

One fact remains the same: every important message is either seen or heard or both. Humans communicate primarily with images and sounds. Touch, smell and taste are delightful senses, but they can send only the most primitive or subtle of messages.

Today, film and television use controlled, concentrated pictures and sounds to send out the most powerful, far-reaching messages ever. Yet, quite often these messages are misdirected, misleading and confusing. Why? Because we, as creators of film and television, confuse the wonderful tools and techniques used to create our messages with the messages themselves. It's so easy and so much fun to create a beautiful package that we sometimes forget to put anything in the box!

I think much of the problem comes from thinking of film and video production as art--as a purely creative, inspirational activity. It's not.

Ninety-nine per cent of what you see at the movies or on television is as close to art as a kitchen chair is to a Picasso.

A painting by Picasso is for hanging on the wall and appreciating; a kitchen chair is for supporting you and keeping you from falling on your behind when you sit down.

Like the craft of chairmaking, the craft of film and television has certain basic rules of construction, and certain observable standards of success. If it supports its occupant, the chair is a success. If your program delivers the right message to the right person, it's a success.

Just as the chairmaker might hope that someday he, like Duncan Phyfe, will craft a chair that surpasses its utility to become art, so we as film and video craftsmen can dream of emulating Orson Welles and creating another "Citizen Kane."

In the meantime, let's make good programs, programs that send clear, understandable messages. To do that, we must understand and control how our viewers react--which is what this book is about.

2. Beginning

Define your goal: how should the viewer react?

Control is the essence of film and television. Unlike others who communicate with images and sound--playwrights, for example--we control totally what our viewer sees and hears; we also control when he sees and hears it. The screen is a window moving through a world that we create. We decide what's in the window, how to show it and when to show it. If we decide wrong, the viewer gets the wrong message or no message.

To control the window properly, we need to aim it toward a clearly defined goal. The goal is your viewer's reaction. <u>A film or video project can have only one goal--to get the viewer to react in a certain way.</u> If you want him to say, "Hey, that was fun to watch!", don't put something in the window that <u>isn't</u> fun to watch. If you do, you'll send the viewer a confusing message.

The screen is a window moving through a world you create.
You control what the viewer sees.

The first thing I do on every project, without exception, is ask the client--even if I'm the client--to describe the intended viewer, the conditions under which he will view the program, and how he should react to the program.

Things I like to know about the viewer are his cultural and educational background, his knowledge of the subject, and why he should want to watch the program.

Will the program be viewed alone or in a group? Will there be a live introduction of the program or a followup discussion? Will related printed materials be available?

What about the viewing room? Will it be airconditioned? Will there be distractions? What size screen will be used? What sort of loudspeakers?

If intended for employees, will the program be viewed on company time or the employee's own time?

Every program, even a mass audience program, has a target viewer who can be defined in some way. For example, the typical viewer of a soap opera differs in many ways from the viewer of a program on investment banking.

You can't know too much about your viewer; he--or she--is the sole reason for your work.

Once you set a goal, never let it go.

Once you know who your viewer is going to be, where he's going to be, and how you want him to react, engrave this information on your forehead. Everything you do from now on hould be with this goal in mind. At every step, ask yourself, "Will this contribute to my goal? Will this make the viewer react the way I want him to? How can I do this in a different way so it works better toward my goal?"

Let's say your program's goal is to explain a very complicated procedure to non-technical people. Should you make a special trip to a distant city to film an intricately detailed mockup of the equipment? Or should you spend the same amount of money on a simple animation sequence? Your client, an engineer, might be very proud of his mockup--and it will probably look better on screen than your animation--but will it explain the procedure better? No. Spend your money on the animation; it will send a more understandable message to the viewer. When in doubt, visualize your viewer looking at the screen; make the program for him.

Make no decision, write no scene, select no location, film no setup, make no cut, without looking ahead and asking, "How will my viewer react to this? Am I on the road to my goal? Is this the best road?"

Does the client really need film or video?

You may feel that a film or video isn't the best way to serve a client's needs and spend his money. Sometimes a pamphlet or a slide show can work just as well, or better. In such a case, you have to decide for yourself what to do.

If you've got overhead to meet and no other work in sight, you might go ahead and take the job. All I can say is, in the long run, I think this will hurt you--without even considering how it will affect the client. You'll put yourself in the position of a car salesman who sells a man a Mercedes Benz when what he really needs and can afford is a Suzuki 4X4. Sooner or later the customer will realize his mistake. You'll have your commission on the Mercedes; but it'll be a cold day in hell before that customer says anything good about you, your company, or the wisdom of buying a Mercedes Benz.

Client contact - one is best.

Ideally, your regular contact person at the client company should be the person with approval authority. As a general rule, the more dispersed the approval authority, the less clearly defined are your goals, and the less successful your program.

When dealing with a number of approvers, what I try to do is have one or more open-ended meetings in which I listen to everybody's ideas and explain what is and what is not possible. Then I write a script or shooting plan and get everyone to approve it. After script approval, I ask that one person be given authority to act for the group from there on in. Then, and only then, do we start preproduction.

It's important that the client understand very clearly what you are going to do and why, and what he's going to end up with. Make sure he understands the cost of changing his mind once the process starts. Most importantly of all, make sure you have a clear idea of your program's goals; make sure that you know exactly who your viewer is and how you want him to react.

3. Scripts

Content is only the beginning.

The viewer reacts to the content or message of your program. If you're writing an original dramatic script, you create 100% of the content; you decide what message to send to your viewer. For most non-dramatic projects, you have less control over content; the program message is, to some extent, predetermined. A dogfood commercial must send the message, "Buy this dogfood." A documentary on African pygmies should say something about pygmies.

Content is only the beginning. There is no such thing as good or bad content in a film or tape; there are only programs that work and programs that don't work. Your program is successful only if you get your content across to your viewer and he reacts to it the way you want him to.

Write for the viewer's reaction.

The purpose of any film or video is to make the viewer react. Design your script with this is mind. In general, you want the viewer to react in one of four ways:

1. you want him to understand what you're explaining;

2. you want him convinced of your argument;

3. you want him to take the action you suggest;

4. you want to entertain him;

Usually you want several of these reactions at the same time.

For example, you might want a mechanic viewing a training film to understand a new work technique. At the same time, you want him convinced of its value to him. In addition, you want him to <u>take action</u> and put the new technique into effect. Furthermore, you want to <u>entertain</u> him enough so that he doesn't fall asleep during the screening.

<u>Establish a style for the project.</u>

Your program delivers a message to the viewer. The way the message is delivered is the program's <u>style</u>. Old-time telegrams also delivered a message; their style was yellow paper, all capital letters, and sentences that ended with "STOP." This made them easy to understand. Your program's style, like a telegram's, should contribute to clear understanding of its message.

The best style is invisible--it works so well in delivering messages that the viewer doesn't even notice it. If your next door neighbor asks, in standard English, to borrow your lawn mower, you understand him perfectly; you don't even think about what language he's speaking. However, let him ask for the same mower in the English of William Shakespeare and suddenly you're more interested in how he talks--his style--than in what he has to say. His style is inappropriate; it distracts the receiver of the message--you--from the message itself--a request to borrow your lawn mower.

<u>An appropriate style delivers the message without distracting.</u>

Just as your neighbor establishes his style when he chooses to speak either modern or 16th century English, so you determine your style by the choices you make, conscious or otherwise, in putting together your program. The script is your first opportunity to do this. Use it to establish a style that fits your viewer. Choose concepts and language that he'll understand without effort. Choose video and sound techniques that he will be comfortable with. Choose actors, locations, props, sequences and other elements that contribute to your viewer's understanding of your program's message.

For example, if you want the viewer of an industrial film to like the company portrayed in the film, establish an appropriate style. Use positive words in your copy. Call for shots that show the factory in the most flattering way: floors swept clean; happy, attractive workers. Specify carefully chosen camera angles that make the offices look spacious and uncrowded. Ask for bright colors and flowers in the frame whenever possible. Call for background music that is upbeat and perky. All these choices make up a style that points the viewer in the direction you want him to go; they contribute to making him react the way you want him to. If your program were an expose of a corrupt industry and you wanted the viewer to dislike the company, this same style (positive and upbeat) would be inappropriate and send a confused, ineffective message to your viewer.

To learn how to write clearly and with appropriate style, read The Elements of Style, by Strunk and White. I review its 85 pages every few months and it always helps me.

Believability - the first priority.

Before anything else, you <u>must</u> make the viewer accept your program's reality. You have to pull him into the world that you are creating. If he stands outside looking in, saying to himself, "This is just a movie," you'll never have his full attention, and you'll never get him to react the way you want him to.

It's easier to get a beginning swimmer into the water if Mommy or Daddy is already there waiting. In the same way, your viewer is more likely to jump into the waters of your program's world if he sees someone--or something--familiar there waiting for him.

<u>To make the viewer believe in your program,</u>
<u>Show someone or something familiar.</u>

Newspaper reporters have used this technique for years--they call it "getting the local angle." Next time you read about a plane crash in the paper, notice the prominence given to local victims. A thousand Pakistanis and one American could die in an earthquake and the <u>Podunk Herald</u> would still lead off with, "Podunk Man Dies In Earthquake." Why? Because the newspaper knows that Podunkians are more interested in one dead man they know than in a thousand dead men they don't know. The one dead Podunkian provides the connection between the reality of Podunk and the reality of a tragedy half-way around the world; it makes the earthquake real for the people of Podunk.

Cartoons and fantasy films are totally unrealistic yet, for as long as they last, we accept the worlds they create. Why? Because there is usually a character we recognize as a familiar type--Will E. Coyote in the Road Runner cartoons, for example, or Luke Skywalker in Star Wars. True, Will is a coyote and Luke is a future space warrior, but they each remind us of someone we've known, or maybe of a part of ourselves. They each stretch out a familiar hand and pull us in.

People are fascinated by things that are familiar and comfortable, yet different. If your viewer can say "Hey, that could be me!" or "I know someone just like that!" then he's accepted your program's reality. A farmer who wouldn't walk across the room to look at the world's rarest fish stands fascinated before a two-headed pig; why? because that could have been his pig!

In the same way, we are much more likely to believe ordinary people than professional spokespersons. When making a documentary or industrial program, use actors whom the viewers can identify with. Most of the time, a celebrity draws attention to himself and away from your message. The exception is when the celebrity is an acknowledged expert on the subject--Paul Newman on race car driving, for example--or a role model, such as a popular TV cop on police procedures.

Experts of any type are always believable. I'd rather learn about a new tool from an experienced mechanic than from a professional actor. A farmer is usually a more believable explainer of his own planting techniques than an actor reading lines.

The one thing you have to watch out for with experts is jargon. Every specialty has its own shorthand way of comunicating. Be sure that your expert uses words that your viewers will easily understand.

Keep your world from falling apart.

Once you've brought your viewer into the world of your program, you must keep that world from falling apart. It's existence hangs on the slender thread of the viewer's belief. The slightest jolt can break that thread and remind the viewer that he's only watching a screen.

The easiest way to jolt the viewer is to tell a lie, be inaccurate. If an actor/doctor uses the wrong instrument, any real doctor watching is going to sit up straight and say, "Hey, that's not right!" Your program has lost him.

Each program must maintain its own internal logic. If you establish that, in your movie, the sky is always green, don't show it blue; you'll remind your viewer that he is being manipulated. He'll take his attention span and go home.

Bad technique will always remind the viewer of the screen and yank him out of the program. For example, showing a man hatless in a wide shot, then cutting to a close shot of the same man with a hat on. Or dubbing a scene so badly that the voice continues for several seconds after the actor's mouth closes.

There may be times when you want to deliberately yank the thread of your viewer's belief, or even break it. Perhaps you want to shake him up and get his attention by deliberately inserting inaccuracies in your program. Or you might want to make him feel uncomfortable and negative toward the contents of your program by showing only unlikable actors. In these cases, you are deliberately making your style--the way you deliver your message--part of the message itself. This can be very effective, if used properly. Just be sure you know what you're doing and how your viewer is going to react.

A frequently used belief-breaker is having an actor in a dramatic scene turn and talk directly to the camera/viewer. This is usually done for comedy effect. The idea is to step outside the movie and comment on it as a movie. This is a sophisticated technique and requires a special, sophisticated audience.

Plan the shape of your program.

A good program has a shape. Its shape is determined by the ebb and flow of your viewer's interest. You want a strong beginning, then a continual movement that builds to a strong end. First you grab the viewer's interest and pull him into the world of your program; then you keep him constantly interested in what's going to happen next until the end, which should be the logical conclusion of all that came before.

Think of the beginning of your program as a fishing trip. You bait your hook with something that will pique the viewer's interest. Then, when he bites, you reel him in. You see good examples of this every night on television. They're called "teasers" or "lead-ins" and are designed to keep you tuned in for upcoming stories. For example:

"Next, our reporter 'cleans up' on the stock market." (A story on what you can learn from the trash left on the floor of the Stock Exchange.)

"Coming up, the arrest of a local 'underground' figure." (The groundskeeper at a local golf course shows a new device to capture gophers.)

A good hook can use pictures or sound or both. For example, begin a tape on tooth care with a super-magnified look at plaque on an average tooth. Start another show in black with doctors' voices discussing an operation; then fade-in to show the discussion is really about office organization. Begin a film on assembly-line techniques with a cut-to-music montage of factory shots. All these examples show the familiar in an unfamiliar way; this is probably the best all-around bait you can use.

Once you have your viewer's interest, you want to keep him with you all the way to the end. In dramatic films, the easiest way is to get the viewer to like your characters and want to know what happens to them. For an educational film, show the viewer a goal that the program will help him reach: "At the end of this program you'll know and understand time and motion study."

You can also maintain viewer interest by setting up a problem, then solving it: "Salesmen who don't use computer projections lose sales. This program will show you how to use the latest computer techniques to increase your sales." Drama is a great viewer-holder, even in non-dramatic programs. Just as your eye will follow a bouncing ball, so your viewer will follow a dramatic development. For example, use suspense to introduce a new technique: "Is this the answer to our problems? Will it work? Let's see." Use surprise: the on-camera spokesman says the new technique is a waste of time--then an ordinary guy comes on and proves otherwise. Use sympathy: an actor/worker thinks he's going to be fired because he can't understand the new technique; then a friend shows him how.

Use texture to keep your viewer interested.

Nothing dulls viewer interest quicker than monotony--the same unchanging picture, the same sound. This is a particular problem with narrated programs. The solution is to add texture, a continually changing and interweaving of different content, sounds and pictures. It's like a lot of little hooks gently pulling the viewer forward.

Give texture to your content by varying it--new ideas, different approaches to old ideas, unexpected concepts.

Give visual texture to your films and videos by continually showing new things, or showing familiar things from new angles. Break up a series of interviews with silent related footage while the interview continues voice-over. Use as many different visual locales as possible.

Give texture to your sound track by using different voices and by switching between sync-sound and voice-over narration. Specify changes in background music to reinforce the mood of the visuals. Call for sound effects and background ambient noise wherever possible. Leave occasional pauses in the narration to hear sound effects, ambience, and music.

Try to avoid hearing only one voice for the entire program. If you must use one voice, try to break away from it from time to time and hear music only, or ambience/sound effects only. When the same voice comes back, even if it's only been gone a few seconds, it will seem fresher.

To get information across, repeat it and link it.

The average viewer remembers clearly only the last ten or fifteen seconds of what he's seen and heard. So, to get information across, repeat it: tell the viewer what you're going to say; say it; then tell him what you said.

Information is conveyed even better if it's repeated in a different way. By doing this you accomplish two things: first, if the information was understood the first time, you reinforce it; secondly, if the information was missed the first time, it might get through when it's repeated in a different way. For example, to get across the idea that smoking kills, first have a doctor say that smoking can kill you, then show the cancerous lungs of a dead smoker.

One technique which is particularly effective is linkage--tying one piece of information to another. For example, to reinforce the message that truck drivers should fasten their seatbelts, you might first show the driver getting in and fastening his belt, while the narrator tells why it's a good idea. Later, in a section on emergency maneuvering, the narrator might mention that the driver has better control of the truck because his seatbelt is fastened.

Think about your budget when you write the script.

If you know how much money there is to spend, you can tailor the script to stretch your dollars as far as possible. You save yourself the agony of rewriting to eliminate sequences, locations, props, equipment and actors that you can't afford. You also save yourself the embarrassment of running out of money before you've finished the program.

The truth is always friendly. Don't be afraid to clearly face all the limitations on your production as early as possible. Think of it as laying out the boundaries of the playing field. Once the lines are clearly laid down, you can play with total confidence; you won't waste time and energy on out-of-bounds balls, and all your goals will count.

If you can afford only one day's work from your principal spokesperson, write his part as a number of small bits scattered throughout the script, connected by narration. You can shoot many short, simple scenes in one day, and still have an hour left over to record the narration. In the final program, the viewer will see and hear the spokesperson as much as if you'd shot a week's worth of complicated on-camera sequences.

If all your actors are going to be non-professionals essentially portraying themselves, don't write a script that calls for them to do or say anything outside their normal experience. If you do, they'll usually come off looking stiff, posed, or self-conscious.

If there's neither the time nor the money to light large interiors, don't write scenes that take place inside airplane hangars at night.

The main thing is to work with what you've got. Don't waste time lamenting what you could do if you had the money. Use what you've got to the absolutely best advantage.

Script formats.

A script is an outline for working. Ideally, you should be able to write it any way you want to, as long as it works for you. However, when other people start working from your script, it's a good idea to use a familiar format that they understand and are comfortable with.

There are two generally used formats: the two-column script, used for TV commercials and most non-fiction work; and the dramatic script. Following are brief examples.

Sample Two-Column Script

(Scene or shot numbers are often not added until you have a
locked-in ready-to-shoot script.)

VIDEO	AUDIO
FADE IN ON	
LAWYER IN OFFICE, WORKING AT DESK	NARRATOR: Joe Goodguy, crusading public servant, burns the midnight oil for the voters of our state.
	(FADE IN PATRIOTIC MARCH MUSIC UNDER NARRATOR)
CLOSE SHOT, JOE ADJUSTS OIL IN DESK LAMP	The light of freedom will never fade while Joe Goodguy is on the job.
FREEZE FRAME, HEROIC POSE OF LAWYER AT DESK	Re-elect Joe Goodguy, Libertarian candidate for Dog Catcher. (MUSIC UP AND OUT)
FADE TO BLACK	

Sample Dramatic Script--Writer's Master Scene Script

(In this first version of the script, concentrate your efforts on content and flow. Give master scene descriptions, with no camera instructions. To focus the camera on a particular subject, list the subject without specifying a camera angle. For example,

    JOE (as shown below)

INTERIOR - NIGHT - LAWYER'S OFFICE

JOE GOODGUY, a young public servant, works at his desk by the light of an oil lamp.

> JOE
> (muttering to himself)
> Boy, do I like working for the public and doing good!

NARRATOR enters the office.

> NARRATOR
> (reverently, with awe)
> Joe, I don't know how you do it. Twenty-four hours a day, every day, working for the public good.

JOE

He adjusts the oil in the lamp on his desk.

> JOE
>
> Aw shucks, Al. I figure it's the least I can do for the privilege of living in a great country like ours.

BACK TO SCENE

> NARRATOR
> (musing, to himself)
>
> God only knows what will happen to our little community if we don't keep this fine Libertarian boy on as County Dog Catcher.

Sample Dramatic Script--Director's Shooting Script

(Once your content is locked in, this is where you as the director add specific camera instructions. The last step, just before actual preproduction begins, is to assign scene numbers.)

FADE IN:

INTERIOR - NIGHT - LAWYER'S OFFICE

JOE GOODGUY,a young public servant, works at his desk by the light of an oil lamp.

                    JOE
          (muttering to himself)
          Boy, do I like working for the
          public and doing good!

As the CAMERA PULLS BACK our NARRATOR enters the frame and approaches JOE's desk.   JOE looks up.

MEDIUM SHOT - NARRATOR - JOE'S P.O.V. (Point-of-view)

                    NARRATOR
          (reverently, with awe)
          Joe, I don't know how you do it.
          Twenty-four hours a day, every
          day, working for the public
          good.

MEDIUM SHOT - JOE - NARRATOR'S P.O.V.

JOE reaches out and adjusts the oil in the lamp on his desk. Patriotic march MUSIC FADES IN under.

                    JOE
          (humbly)

          Aw shucks, Al. I figure it's
          the least I can do for the
          privilege of living in a great
          country like ours.

CLOSE SHOT - NARRATOR - DIFFERENT ANGLE

The NARRATOR turns away from JOE'S desk and faces the camera.

CONTINUED

                    NARRATOR
                (musing, to himself)

        God only knows what will
        happen to our little community
        if we don't keep this fine
        Libertarian boy on as County
        Dog Catcher.

He looks back at JOE at his desk.

MEDIUM SHOT - JOE AT DESK

He continues to work diligently, pausing
occasionally to wipe sweat from his brow.
Patriotic march MUSIC SWELLS.

                            FADE OUT

_____

     If your script mixes non-fiction and dramatic segments, you

might want to mix the two formats. Or, if neither format serves

your particular needs, invent your own. The important thing is

to clearly and completely set down your ideas for the program.

4. Preproduction

"When a man's knowledge is not in order, the more of it he has, the greater will be his confusion of thought," Herbert Spencer.

"To foresee is to rule," Blaise Pascal.

Use a production board.

Once you have a script or a program outline, you can start organizing for the shoot. I use a production board. (See page 34 for how to make or buy one.)

"MY MOVIE"		4	8	3	9	11	24	1	22				
Dir: Tom		H O M E	H O M E	C A R	C A R	C A R	C A R	J O B	J O B				
Prod: MGM		--	--	--	--	--	--	--	--	--			
		S y n c	S y n c					S y n c	S y n c				
		--	--	--	--	--	--	--	--	--	--		
		1 hr	2 hr	1+ 1/ 2 hr	1/ 2 hr	3/ 4 hr	3/ 4 hr	1 hr	2+ 1/ 2 hr				
		--	--	--	--	--	--	--	--	--	--		
1 Mary	1		1	1	1	1	1						
2 Joe	2	2			2	2	2	2	2				
3 Dog	3	3	3										
4 Porsche	4			4	4								
5 Crane	5	5											
6	6												

Scene number — Location — Individual Strips — Divider Strips

Upper left-hand corner of a production board

A production board is a frame that holds loose vertical strips of thick posterboard. On the left is a header board--a wide strip of posterboard with forty or so numbered lines. On the lines, you write the names of all your actors, extras, props, vehicles, special camera equipment, and anything else that's important.

Next, you go through your script and make up a separate strip for each scene. The scene number and location go at the top. In the same space, I often add whether the scene is sync-sound and how much time I think it will take to shoot. (On feature films, it's customary to write the number of script pages.) I also use transparent marking pens to color code the top of the strips: clear for day exterior, green for day interior, blue for night exterior, and red for night interior. If you want, you can use colored strips for the same purpose.

As I make up each new strip, I put it in the board at the far left next to the header board listing my actors, props and so on. Then I go down the strip and write the number of each element needed in that scene. As I come across elements not yet listed, I add them.

Work from most difficult to least difficult.

When I have all my scenes converted to production strips, I start shuffling the strips around. First I group the strips according to location. Then I organize each location group according to day or night, interior or exterior. After that, what I do varies with the situation. If I have one actor who is available only in the morning, then I'll group all his scenes together. If I'm renting an expensive camera crane, I'll try to do all the crane shots at the same time.

I use black separator strips--or any other color I'm not using--to group the strips into working days and locations.

The general rule is to order your work from most difficult to least difficult, from most expensive to cheapest. For example, if your program takes place in a large office, shoot all the wide shots first. Then shoot progressively smaller scenes. This accomplishes two purposes. First, it's always easier to move lights and equipment in to a smaller area; moving in, you always have a clean, lit area in front of the camera; moving out, you have to rig extra lights and clean up what moments before was a behind-the-camera work area.

The second reason to work from large to small is to use your actors and extras most efficiently. If you shoot all the big scenes together, you will need the majority of your actors for a lot less time than if they stand around while you shoot scenes they aren't in.

The production board forces you to consider all your needs and how they affect each other. For example, if the board shows one location where half the scenes are day exteriors and the other half are interiors that require lights, you see immediately the advantage of shooting the exteriors first while your lighting crew sets up inside.

Production boards are usually associated with theatrical movies. I think this is a mistake. They've helped me tremendously on industrial and documentary programs. For example, I made a film on computer furniture that involved a large office set and many different actor/extras. Using my production board, I planned the shooting so that, as well as working from large to small setups, I could film each actor within minutes of his arrival, then dismiss him. Everything should have gone like clockwork. It did, until two actors failed to appear and a piece of furniture didn't work as advertised.

With the production board, I was able to clearly see all my remaining requirements, then quickly rearrange the shooting schedule, confident that nothing would fall through the cracks in the shuffle.

For complicated projects, you will probably want to prepare breakdown sheets first, then transfer the information to the production board. Breakdown sheets are forms containing the same information as production board strips, plus extra space for notes. They're used by the production manager and the assistant director to actually arrange for everything to come together.

If you have a large paper cutter, you can make your own production board and strips from cardboard and heavy poster paper. The main requirement is a lip at the top and the bottom to keep the strips from falling out. You can buy large, folding production boards, strips, and breakdown sheets from vendors of motion picture and television supplies. One place you can always find them is Enterprise Printers & Stationers, 7401 Sunset Boulevard, Hollywood, California 90046.

Make sure your assistants know your goals.

On all but the smallest projects, you'll have to delegate some of the preproduction responsibilities: location scouting, set construction, prop rentals, and so on. The surest way to be disappointed by someone doing a job for you is to send that person out without a clear understanding of what you want. For example, a cowboy costume for a comical sequence would be very different from a cowboy costume for a serious historical sequence.

Take the time to explain to each person the goal of your project as it pertains to that person's task. The time spent will pay big dividends.

Cast for believability and self-confidence. Be nice.

Casting the right person for a part is a specialty. For big projects a casting director is well worth the money.

As a general rule, look for believability; if the viewer believes in your actors, he'll be more likely to believe in your program.

Try to find actors that look and sound as close to the part as possible. Really good actors can assume any character; still, the closer they are to the character to begin with, the more likely you are of getting the portrayal you want. Avoid distracting the viewer with unusual accents, hairdos, makeup or clothes, unless specifically required by the script.

When selecting non-actors to participate in a program, look for eagerness and self-confidence. If an employee, nominated by his boss to be in a program, is very nervous about the prospect, do a simple "screen test" with him; have him act out a small scene from the program. Coach him. If he's still clearly unsure of himself, find a way to ease him into a lesser role, or use him as a consultant.

Sometimes company presidents feel as if they're obligated to appear on camera, even when they're uncomfortable doing so. Often, they're relieved when an expert--you--tells them they'll be better served by letting someone else do the talking. This is dangerous ground, though, so be _very_ diplomatic. One approach

I've used is to emphasize the amount of time the production will take them away from their more important duties. I also remind them that, by remaining outside the production, they will be able to more objectively evaulate and critique the program.

Please remember that actors, professional or not, are individuals with feelings. Don't waste their time. Be as specific as possible in your casting; call in only people who are real possibilities. Schedule your interviews so that no one has to wait very long. When you finish an interview, be specific; if an actor is definitely not right for the part, say so then. If you say you'll let them know within a specificed time, <u>do it</u>! (It's usually easier to tell the actors that if they haven't heard from you by a certain date, then they can assume they were not chosen.) Thank each person for coming in. Even though you might not use an actor on this particular show, you may need him or her another time. Actors are like anyone else; they do their best work for people who are courteous and professional.

5. Directing and Shooting

Directing is selecting with style.

As a director, you're responsible for directing or channeling the program so that the viewer reacts the way you want him to. That's your goal.

More than a director, you're a selector. Like a chef shopping for just the right ingredients, you select the pictures and sounds to present to your viewer. Make the right selections, and your program will cause the viewer to react correctly. Make the wrong selections, and your pictures and sounds will cause the viewer to react incorrectly; he'll get audio-visual indigestion. For best results, select pictures and sounds that suit your viewer, that fit within an appropriate style.

Style is the way you communicate, separate from what you communicate. It's the framework within which the director works.

While the scriptwriter outlines the program's style by his choice of concepts and language and scenes and situations, the director determines the program's final overall style by selecting the sights and sounds that will actually communicate the program's message to the viewer.

Excepting those occasions--like perfume commercials and music videos--when the style is the message, the best style is transparent, so perfectly conveying the program's content that the viewer gets the message, but is unaware of how he got it. A style becomes transparent when it matches the viewer's level of audio-visual literacy.

Audio-visual literacy is like reading literacy, except it deals with pictures and sounds. Our reading literacy is determined by the words and grammar that we've learned. In the same way, our audio-visual literacy is determined by the personal library of pictures and sounds and techniques that we know and understand.

Your job as a director is to determine the level of audio-visual literacy of your viewer, then match the style of your program to it. Communicate with pictures and sounds that your viewer will readily understand. Just as a strange new word or sentence construction in a novel will confuse the reader, so a strange new picture or sound or technique in a film will confuse the viewer.

To explain irrigation techniques to a primitive farmer, a simple style is best: the camera at eye level, normal lenses, long intervals between cuts, familiar settings and tools, simple language. To interest a fashion designer in the possibilities of a new fabric, use a much more sophisticated style: quick cuts to music, strange angles and colors, lots of abstract swirling and bending, exotic models. In each case, the viewer gets the message loud and clear, without concerning himself as to how he got it. Why? Because the style of each program matches the audio-visual literacy of its viewer. Imagine the results if you addressed the farmer in fashion-designer style, and vice versa.

<u>To deliver a clear message, match your style to your viewer.</u>

Sometimes, for a special effect, style deliberately intrudes. Comedy programs speed up the action just to be silly. Romantic films slow things down to suggest a beautiful time lasting forever. Investigative news programs shoot faces in uncomfortably tight closeups to increase tension. Using style in this way strengthens the program message; the style actually becomes part of the message. As a general rule, however, the more a viewer notices and remembers your style--how you sent the message--the less he'll remember the message itself.

<u>Take charge.</u>

Once you have a script, you as director should take full and complete charge of the project. Consult with others, get advice from your cameraperson, listen to <u>anybody</u> who has an idea to make the program better, but keep total control to yourself. Make all the final decisions yourself, with your program goal clearly in mind.

Most great enterprises are the work of individuals, either working alone or leading others. There are few statues erected in honor of committees. Committees are best at criticizing and presenting different points of view, not creating.

Sharing the responsibility of directing stifles your creativity. Once immersed in a program, you often work on instinct. The more you have to articulate to someone else the reasoning behind your decisions, the more you stop making decisions you can't or don't have time to articulate. Your work slows down; it gets safe and mushy.

Have a plan, even if it's a bad one.

The best time to plan things out is before you start shooting. The production board, discussed in the previous chapter, is a big help.

Try to always have some kind of plan in mind, even if it's a bad one. At least it'll give you someplace to start; you can always make modifications later. When working in unstructured, uncontrolled situations, it's especially important to have some idea of what you want to accomplish. A plan helps you see more clearly which factors you can and cannot control.

Often you have more control than you realize. Say you have to wait around for a quick walking interview with a politician, then rush it on the air. If you plan for the elements you'll need, you can use the waiting time to shoot your reporter walking along and asking questions. You can also shoot scenes related to the interview: if the subject is the new courthouse, get a couple shots of it. These extra scenes will not only make editing your last minute interview easier; they will make it more interesting and informative.

Storyboards--drawings of your shots--can help you visualize your work. They can also make it easier to explain to other people what you plan to do. Storyboards are used frequently in preparing television commercials, which usually have to be explained to many, many people. You can make perfectly useful storyboards with simple stick drawings. For beginning directors, making up a storyboard is like a free practice shoot.

When you first arrive at a location, walk all around; look at it from every possible angle--high, low, inside, outside, upside down. Continually repeat to yourself your program's goal; think about how you want your particular viewer to react. Select pictures and sounds that will get your message across. Never discard any possiblity of a shot until you've considered it through the eyes of your viewer.

Once you decide what you're going to do, tell everyone. Not just the actors and your assistant and the lighting person. Tell everybody on the set what you're going to do, why you're doing it, and how each person fits into the plan. People who know and understand the purpose of their work do better work. If a production assistant has a better idea, use it; make it your own. Be open, but stay in charge.

You'll find you work better and faster if you keep equipment and people to the bare minimum. Keep your working area clear of everything that is not absolutely essential. As I suggested in the chapter on preproduction, work from the most complicated setup to the least complicated, from the most people to the fewest.

Finally, just because you have a plan, don't get married to it; stay flexible. If things start going wrong, stop; step back as far as you can and look things over. Modify your plan to meet new conditions, or make an entirely new plan.

Color and light

The most important thing to know about color and light is that the viewer's eye automatically focuses on the whitest or brightest area of your frame; ideally, then, this area should coincide with where you want the viewer to look. Don't make your viewer guess what's important; put a spotlight on it.

Warm colors--red, yellow, orange--communicate excitement and warmth; they call attention to themselves. Cool colors--blue and its shades--communicate calm and coolness, even gloom; they're uninviting. Green relaxes.

You'll rarely have a frame composed of just one color group; still, it pays to keep the effects of color in mind. For example, if you must choose between two office locations, one decorated in cool or neutral colors, the other in warm colors, base your decision on how you want your viewer to react. Choose the reddish office if you want the viewer to feel positively about the location; choose the bluish office if you want a more neutral or negative reaction. The difference in effect is subtle, but important.

Color intensity also has an effect on your viewer. Fill the frame with varied, bright colors and you'll communicate happiness and optimism. Fill it with muted, dull colors and you'll send a message of dullness and depression.

If the colors in the frame tell your viewer one thing, and the contents something else, the viewer receives a confused message. The best examples of this are scenes of tropical poverty and war. It is difficult to accept the reality of starving children or dead bodies when they are presented in frames filled with bright and varied colors. The next time you see such a scene on television, turn off the color on your set; notice how the pictures seem more powerful and appropriate.

Lighting

There are two basic approaches to lighting: the classic approach, and the natural source approach. Classic lighting consists of the following: a main or key light to one side and above the subject; a smaller light on the opposite side partially filling in the shadows from the key light; a back light hitting the subject from behind to create a separating halo; and finally a background light illuminating the background. There may or may not be real light fixtures on the set.

The natural source approach consists of placing lights only where they might be in reality. If the sole light source on the set is a table lamp, then additional light needed for film or video is obtained by placing a stronger light off camera on the same level and axis as the lamp. Any additional lighting is done so as to appear to be wall or ceiling reflections of the lamplight.

Classic lighting gives you the freedom to place your lights where they best illuminate your subject. It can, however, look artificial and forced.

Natural source lighting makes the world of your program look more like reality. However, it can severely limit your options and literally leave too much of your picture in the dark.

For most situations, a combination of the two styles works best. Unless the lighting is totally inappropriate in style, I really don't think the average viewer notices where the light comes from. The important thing is that the viewer see what you want him to see.

Traditionally, comedy calls for well-lit sets, with few shadows; drama and suspense work best with more shadow areas.

I usually start off with a natural source approach, then add whatever other lights I need to show everything I want to show. For example, in large offices I begin by bouncing lights off the ceiling, since that's where the natural lighting comes from. With nothing but top light, however, everyone on camera has ugly shadows under their cheekbones and noses; so I add some front light to fill in the faces. I do avoid any hard shadows on walls or desks, as this would be unnatural in a large office setting. In more dramatic locations, I come closer to classic lighting.

Once I have a set lit, I start turning lights off to see if I can do without them. More often than not, fewer lights looks better and gives more depth and texture to the set.

When lighting for video, the most important tool you can have is a properly adjusted monitor to judge your colors on. If you work with anything less, you're handicapping yourself. A wave-form monitor is also a big help.

To ensure that copies of your film or tape have the same
color balance as the original, put color bars at the beginning of
each tape roll and a color bar chart at the head of each film
roll.

A comfortable frame equals a comfortable viewer.

Just as your bedroom window looks out on the reality of your
world, so the viewer's window--the camera frame--looks out on the
reality of your program. If whatever the viewer sees in the
window seems comfortable being there, then you have a good, non-
tense composition, one that doesn't distract the viewer from the
program itself.

For people shots, a loose head-and-shoulders framing is the
most comfortable to look at. The subject is easily recognized
and looks comfortable within the limits of the screen; there's no
danger of him popping out into the viewer's personal space.

A comfortable frame equals a comfortable viewer.

To add tension to a program, put something in the viewer's window that doesn't fit, that looks uncomfortable, such as a composition that chops off part of an important element (like a person's eyes, their head, a pointing arm). Or show something unexpected, such as a giant human eyeball or a view down the edge of the Empire State Building.

Bad camerapersons unintentionally create tension by shooting handheld, instead of putting the camera on a tripod. A shaky handheld camera frame distracts the viewer and yanks him out of the reality of the program.

ARGGH!

<u>An uncomfortable frame equals an uncomfortable viewer</u>

<u>The establishing shot is the what-to-expect shot.</u>

Ideally, when your viewer looks through that window into your program, the first thing he should see is an establishing shot.

The establishing shot defines your program's world for the viewer. It lays down the screen geography--where everything is.

Once you show the viewer a map of your world, you can move him around in it and he won't get confused or lost.

The establishing shot shows where everything is.

For example, after showing a wide shot--an establishing shot--of a classroom, you can show a closeup of the teacher talking and be sure that the viewer knows that this is a teacher in a classroom talking to a group of students. You can show closeups of pencils writing on paper and textbooks being opened and be sure they'll be recognized for what they are by the viewer. In editing, you can rearrange these shots--maybe start with a close-up of a pencil and the sound of the teacher's voice to pique the viewer's interest--but you'll still need to show the establishing shot soon; without it, the viewer will spend too much time wondering where he is and not enough time thinking about what you're telling him.

Beginners often make the mistake of thinking that an establishing shot has to be a wide shot. Not true. An establishing shot should do just that--establish for the viewer where he is in your program's world. If your sequence is about insect antennae, the establishing shot could be a full shot of an ant. If you're talking about space travel, you might want to establish with a shot of the Milky Way. If all the viewer needs to know about a particular sequence is that it shows a man reading at home, then the establishing shot need only be a medium shot of a man, a chair, and a lamp.

Sometimes a series of related shots can substitute for one wide establishing shot. A closeup of hands working on a shoe followed by a closeup of a man looking down can easily establish that he is repairing shoes. In a situation like this, without a wider shot to orient the viewer, it's important to shoot more of each closeup; then the editor can leave it on the screen long enough for the viewer to perceive what is happening. This is a good example of intentional style. The purpose here might be to glamorize the shoe repairman's work by deliberately showing only dramatic closeups.

Sound can help establish your program's reality. For example, a wide shot of a brick building, accompanied by a voice saying, "Good morning, students," immediately tells the viewer that he's looking at a school. A close shot of a person swaying slightly, with train sounds in the background, tells the viewer that he's looking at a railroad passenger.

Basic sequence.

No matter how good your establishing shot, sooner or later your viewer is going to get tired of looking at it. You'll have to show another shot, and another after that. This is editing. Since everything you shoot is going to be edited, it makes sense to shoot with editing in mind. Editing starts with the basic sequence.

The basic sequence is, as its name suggests, the basic building block of the editing process. A minimal basic sequence consists of two related shots that can be arranged and rearranged to lengthen, shorten, and change the emphasis of your message.

Many TV news interviews are minimal basic sequences. They consist of a closeup of the interviewee and a closeup of the reporter. With these two shots, the editor can shorten a half-hour interview to just the first and last comments: he simply cuts out the middle of the interview, then covers the cut with a shot of the reporter listening. Or the editor can rearrange the order of the interview by starting with a shot of the reporter asking the last question, cut to the interviewee's answer, then cut to the reporter's first question, and that answer.

A minimal basic sequence

The important thing--and what gives the editor so much flexibility--is that the two shots, while related in subject matter, are independent of each other visually; you don't see the reporter in the interviewee's shot, and you don't see the interviewee in the reporter's shot. This means you can cut back and forth between then without worrying about matching visual elements, such as arm and hand positions. The shot that makes this possible is that of the reporter--the <u>cutaway</u>. It's purpose is to provide an easy way to "cut away" from the main shot of the interviewee talking.

For maximum flexibility in editing, you should have more than two shots in a basic sequence. Shoot a wide establishing shot, a medium shot and a closeup of your main subject, plus at least one cutaway. Wide, medium and close are relative terms. A wide shot should show everything that's important, and nothing more. The medium and close shots show progressively less.

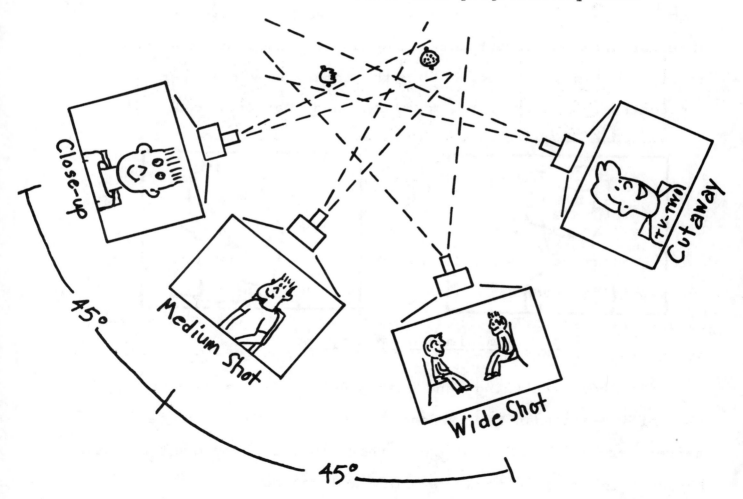

<u>Camera placement for basic sequence (from above)</u>

To lessen your dependence on the cutaway, move the camera 45 degrees or more between shots of your main subject. This makes it easier to cut directly between them; the angle change disorients the viewer slightly and distracts from any change in your subject's position from one shot to the next. When shots cut together easily, with nothing to distract the viewer, the sequence is said to have good continuity.

Edited basic sequence

Basic sequences are not limited to interviews, nor are cutaways limited to shots of reporters. A basic sequence of a man repairing a car could use a shot of the man's face as a cutaway from his hands working on the engine. The clock on the garage wall, or the garage dog scratching, could also be cutaways.

Any shot can be a cutaway, as long as it relates in some way to the main shot, without having to match anything in the main shot. To cut away from the mechanic's hands working, you could use an extreme wide shot of the mechanic in which you don't see his hands down inside the car.

Overlapping action / clean entrances and exits

Say you shoot a wide shot of a woman sitting down at a desk; then you move your camera around 45 degrees for the medium shot of her at work. The transition between the two shots will be smoother if, at the beginning of the medium shot, you have her repeat the action of sitting down. This is called overlapping the action between the two shots. The editor can then cut from wide shot to medium shot as the woman sits down. The viewer's eye will follow the sitting movement and not notice the cut. This is called cutting on the action.

Let's say the woman talks on the phone for a while, hangs up, and takes an envelope from her IN basket. Frame your camera on the IN basket, then have the woman's hand enter and remove the envelope completely from the frame. This is called a clean entrance and clean exit and is very useful, because this shot now exists independently from the rest of the sequence. You can cut to the shot of the basket before the hand enters, then wait until the hand exits with the envelope before cutting to another shot. Since the hand is not in the shot of the IN basket when you cut, you don't have to match the exact positions of the fingers and arm in the surrounding shots. This makes editing much easier.

A clean entrance and exit can also serve as a cutaway to jump forward past other actions that you might want to eliminate. For example, to eliminate the woman's initial phone conversation, cut away from the medium shot before she picks up the phone, go to the shot of the IN basket, have her hand enter, pick up the envelope and exit, then cut back to the medium shot of her studying the contents of the envelope.

Crossing the line.

The line, also called the axis of action, is an imaginary line that indicates the direction people and things face when viewed through the camera. When you cross the line with the camera, you reverse the screen direction of your subjects. This confuses the viewer.

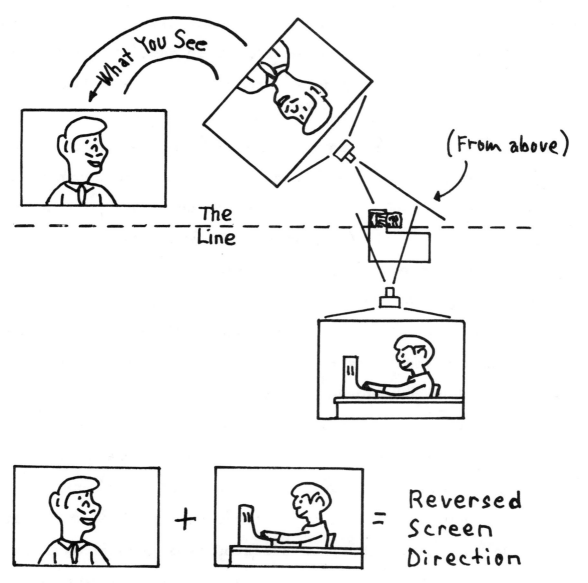

Crossing the line reverses your screen direction.

You'll never have trouble with crossing the line if you always keep things facing the same direction when seen through the camera. If you're shooting a sequence of Man A, make a mental note that he is looking to screen left; every time you move the camera, make sure A is still looking screen left.

You can cross the line and not confuse the viewer. One way is to have the subject reverse direction while the camera is running, such as filming a horse as it races around a track. Another way is to physically move the camera across the line from one side of your subject to the other, while the camera is running. This is frequently done with a dolly, a wheeled camera platform.

In editing, you can cross the line if you stop on it; between two shots of the same subject with opposite screen directions, insert a shot looking straight down the line, neither left nor right. For example, start with a wide shot of a car moving down the street from left to right, cut to a shot of the car coming directly at the camera, then cut to a different shot of the car from the other side of the street. It's now traveling from right to left on the screen. The neutral head-on shot serves as a bridge to reverse the car's screen direction without jarring the viewer. A point-of-view shot looking through the windshield from inside the car would work just as well.

Finally, you can jump back and forth across the line within a sequence if you include in your shots some visual element with a clearly defined direction. This serves as a geographical reference point and compass for the viewer. For example, a lunch counter with customers on one side only, a sidewalk with street traffic on one side, or a concert stage.

<u>Shooting is preparing to edit.</u>

Once you start editing, you will rarely have the chance to go back and shoot forgotten cutaways, or to overlap actions to smooth a cut, or to shoot clean entrances and exits. Plan your shooting with editing in mind.

If you have any time at all, shoot a basic sequence, even if it's only one main shot and one cutaway, or a wide shot and a close-up from two different angles.

Slate your shots. A slate is simply an identification at the beginning of a picture or sound recording. It can be a professional camera slate, a piece of paper--even a voice on the videotape. In editing, slates make it easier to find and keep track of your material.

If you have an assistant cameraperson, have him or her keep a camera log, a list of all your takes in the order they're shot. On the log, note anything you think is important, like elapsed time of the take, videotape time code, lens focal length, camera moves, variations in the action, and so on. Circle the number of the best take or takes of each scene. If you record sound-only on videotape, note your sound recordings on the same log.

When shooting unscripted footage, slate your shots sequentially: 1, 2, 3 and so on, to the end of the production. With each shot having its own number and description, you'll find it simpler to organize your material for editing.

It's much easier to edit dramatic sequences when you know exactly which shots cover which dialogue and action. As you shoot, this information can be quickly noted on your script. The following two pages show how I prepare script notes.

56

32A - MASTER - 16mm - from door toward sun porch, sofa in
          foreground - T1 T2 (T3)

32B - 50mm - MS Sarah - Jason and couch off camera - (T1) T2 T3
          T4 (T5)

32C - 16mm - low wide angle Jason in profile in foreground, Sarah
          in background - T1 T2 (T3) T4 T5 T6 T7 (T8)✳

32D - 50mm - CU Sarah from Jason's POV - T1 T2 T3 (T4)

32E - 50mm - CU Jason from Sarah's POV - T1 T2 T3 (T4)

Script notes:

    Solid vertical lines on the script indicate what each shot
covers. A squiggly line indicates off-camera dialogue or action
not seen in that particular shot.

    Detailed descriptions of the camera shots are written (as
shown above) to the left, on the back of the previous page. I
circle the good takes. When one take is best among several good
ones, I star its circle. Feel free to modify the system to your
own needs.

32A

32B

32C

32D

32E

32. INTERIOR - DAY - LIVING ROOM

JASON is asleep on the couch. SARAH enters
quickly from the sun porch, slamming the
door, then stops abruptly when she sees
JASON.

                    JASON
               (half asleep)
          Huh? Whuzzat?

                    SARAH
          Sorry, I wasn't aware there
          was anyone in here.

                    JASON
          Thassalright. Iwuz jus
          layin...

JASON tries to stand up, then falls back
down on the couch. SARAH turns away in
disgust.

                    SARAH
          Didn't you promise Mother
          you'd stop drinking? You sot!
          You disgusting, reprehensible
          drunk!

JASON finally sits up.

                    JASON
          Thass one way of puttin it,
          I s'ppose.

SARAH walks over and looms over him.

                    SARAH
          How could you? How could you?
          Don't you care about anybody
          but yourself?

JASON holds his head in his hands. He sighs
deeply.

                    JASON
          Uh, uh, uh...

He falls back on the couch, unconscious.
Disgusted, SARAH walks back out onto the
sun porch, slamming the door behind her.

On-camera talent.

   The theatrical director is continually fighting to keep his audience's attention focused where he wants it. He calls attention to particular areas of the stage with special lighting and with the exaggerated gestures and voices of his actors,

   The director of a film or video program, on the other hand, has total control of what his audience sees and hears. The camera frame and the sound track are his primary pointers, not the actors.

   The film and video actor, therefore, can perform in a more natural, unforced manner than his theatrical counterpart. He can concentrate completely on becoming his character; the director will worry about getting, and keeping, the viewer's attention.

   The two most important things a director can do for an actor are to make him comfortable and to explain the program goals to him. With actors, you're more a motivator than a director. Just as a coach can only guide his team from the sidelines, so a director can only cheer on the actors from behind the camera. You'll get your best results with positive, upbeat guidance.

   Acting is delicate work, and each actor has his own working method. Give respect to the actor as a fellow craftsman. Explain as best you can how you want your viewer to react to his performance; point the actor toward your goal, then let him get there in his own way.

   Your main concern is that the viewer not be aware of the actors "acting." You want him to believe that the people on the screen are real. With actors who have recently worked on the stage, ask for less energy than normal, especially in closeups.

Educational and industrial programs often use non-actors to portray either themselves or people like themselves. Don't expect these non-profesionals to act. Think more in terms of documenting their normal actions. Make them think in those terms, too, and they'll be more relaxed and natural in front of the camera.

Professionals can act out emotions; amateurs can't, so don't expect them to. Ask non-professional actors for behavior: don't ask them to be happy; ask them to smile. Don't ask a non-pro for self-confidence; ask him to stand straight and speak strongly and clearly.

It's very important that non-professional actors feel totally comfortable and confident on the set. Take the time to introduce them to your crew and to explain each person's function. Demonstrate your equipment; let them look through the camera and listen through the headphones. Take all the mystery out of the situation; get across the idea that, just like them, you're only doing a job.

If your lighting and other setups are complicated and time-consuming, it's a good idea to keep non-professionals away from the set altogether until they're needed. You don't want them to think about all the preparation focusing on them. Also, a casual remark by a crew member about a technical problem can be blown out of proportion in the mind of a non-pro. Or worse, the non-professional can pick up just enough knowledge to start question-ing and interfering in areas beyond his expertise.

<u>Cueing the talent.</u>

There are three ways for actors to deliver long speeches directly to the camera: memorize the copy, use a Teleprompter, or use cue cards.

Memorized copy is best, <u>if</u> the actor can speak convincingly without a vacant-eyed search for each new line. It places a heavy responsibility on the actor.

Teleprompters are convenient but bulky. A Teleprompter consists of a TV monitor hung face up on the front of the camera; a two-way mirror in front of the camera lens reflects the monitor's screen out to the actor. This enables the actor to look directly at the lens and read the copy as it scrolls up the screen. The copy is either electronically generated or typed on sheets which move on a conveyor belt past a camera.

Teleprompters are heavy; they limit camera movement. They are also relatively expensive. If you use a Teleprompter be sure to keep it far enough away from the talent so that his eyes don't dart noticeably from left to right as he reads each line.

The most common cueing method is cue cards. Make cue cards by cutting 22" x 28" white poster paper in half vertically, yielding two 14" x 22" cards. Use these cue cards vertically, to minimize left-to-right eye movement. Print the copy with thick black marking pens. Use upper and lower case letters; these are easier to read. Number the cards on the back. Hold the cards as close as possible to one side of the camera lens. As the actor reads a card, move it up so that the current line is always opposite the lens, keeping the actor's eye-line at a constant level. As each card ends, the following card should be revealed behind it, already in position. The cue card person should hand used cards to an assistant or quietly drop them on the floor.

It pays to be nice.

It's my personal opinion that courtesy, even kindliness, pays off for the director. I've already spoken of the importance of making actors comfortable and confident. Now I'll go further: I think you should treat everybody on the set nice. Keep everyone fully informed of what you're doing and why. Make everybody a part of your team. Informed, friendly people do better work; plus there's the added bonus of the useful hints and suggestions that you'd never get from an uninformed bunch of strangers.

One thing. Don't mistake kindliness for weakness. Be friendly but firm in keeping the program on the road to your goal. Still, if you let your actors and crew know where the production is heading, you should have no trouble leading them there.

Keep your mind on your viewer.

If you as the director have only one thing on your mind, it should be a vision of your viewer reacting to the program. Judge everything you do against this image.

If you want to shoot strange camera angles, fine. But think about your viewer; if there's the slightest doubt he won't get your message, give him an establishing shot first, or hold that unusual shot long enough for him to understand what it is.

When shooting in uncontrolled circumstances, thinking about your viewer is even more important. Ask yourself at each shot, "How do I want the viewer to react to this? What can I do differently to get my message to him? Can I get other shots that will help him understand?"

If you as the director pay constant attention to your viewer, you'll have a better chance of your viewer paying attention to your program.

6. Sound

Vibrating bodies create spherical sound waves.

The sounds we speak are created by air from our lungs,
passing over and vibrating the vocal cords in our necks. Every
sound, whether it be a human voice or a tree falling in the
forest, is caused by something vibrating. When an object
vibrates, it moves back and forth in the surrounding air,
creating waves which move outward, very similar to waves rippling
away from fingers wiggling in a pond. The main difference is
that while water waves travel outward horizontally on the pond
surface, sound waves travel outward in all directions,
spherically.

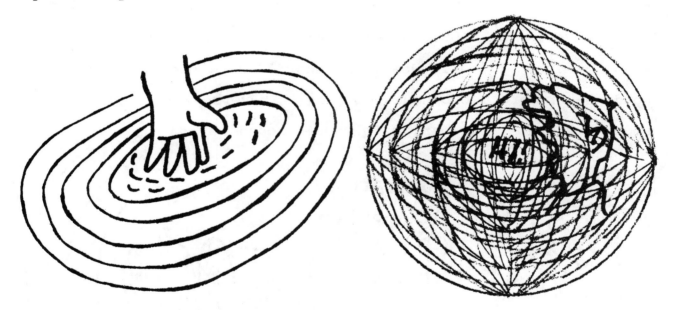

Water waves travel horizontally.
Sound waves travel spherically outward from the source.

The human eardrum is a thin membrane which vibrates when
sound waves reach it. These vibrations are converted to nerve
impulses and sent to the brain, where they are translated into
sounds we "hear."

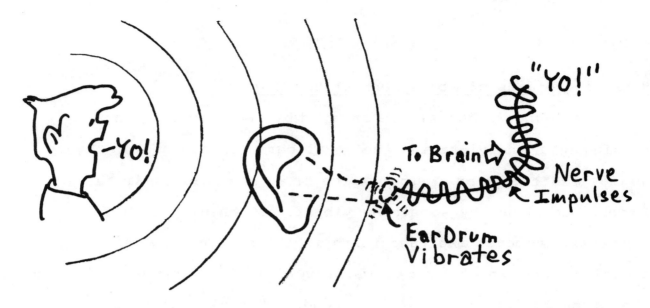

We "hear" the vibrations caused by sound waves.

Microphones are imitations of our ears. Every microphone has an "eardrum", called a diaphragm, which vibrates when hit by sound waves. The vibrations are then converted to an electrical signal which can be broadcast or recorded onto magnetic tape. Loudspeakers are microphones working in reverse: electric signals vibrate a diaphragm to create sound waves.

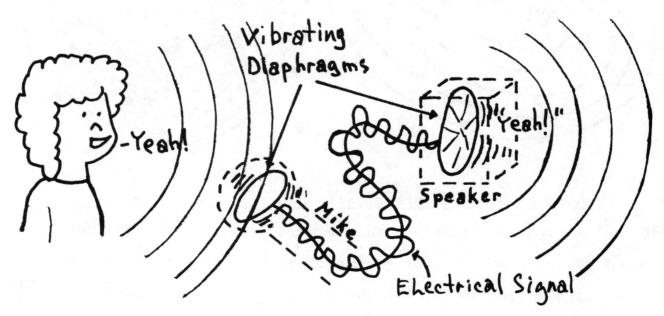

Microphones and loudspeakers imitate the human ear.

The ear, and the microphone, can tell one sound from another by how close together the sound waves occur, and how big they are. The closeness of the waves is called the sound frequency; the size is called amplitude, which we perceive as loudness.

Sound frequency is measured in the number of complete waves, or cycles, that occur each second. Since the words "cycles per second" are not the same in all languages, it was decided to express frequency in Hertz, abbreviated Hz. (Hertz was a German physicist who discovered electromagnetic waves.) 60 Hz means 60 cycles or sound waves per second.

The lower the number of waves or cycles per second, the lower or deeper the sound. The higher the sound frequencey, the shriller the sound. The average person can hear sounds from around 16 Hz to approximately 16,000 Hz. Human speech uses the frequencies between 200 Hz and 8000 Hz, with most of the significant sounds occurring between 200 Hz and 2700 Hz, the range that is transmitted by a typical telephone.

The more sound waves per second--the higher the frequency-- the shriller the sound.

The size of a sound wave--its amplitude--is determined by the intensity of the energy which creates it. As with pond waves, if you hit the water hard, you make a bigger wave; so if you shout you make a bigger sound wave than if you whisper. Our ears perceive the amplitude of a sound wave as loudness.

Sound intensity or loudness is measured in decibels, abbreviated dB. Most audio equipment uses VU (Volume Unit) meters to indicate the strength of a sound signal, as measured in dB. 0 dB on a VU meter is set at a scientifically determined sound level--close to where the average human can just not hear a 1000 Hz tone. Each increase of 3 dB indicates a doubling of the sound intensity. So 6 dB is twice as loud as 3 dB and 9 dB is four times as loud as 3 dB.

Microphones

Film and video productions commonly use two basic types of microphones: dynamic, and electret condenser. Both have diaphragms or membranes that vibrate when hit by sound waves. Both then convert the vibrations into electrical signals.

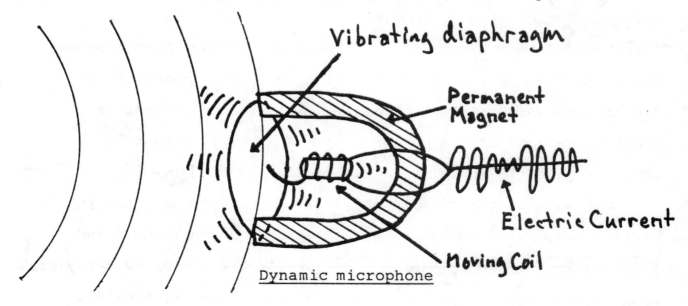

Vibrating diaphragm

Permanent Magnet

Electric Current

Moving Coil

Dynamic microphone

In a dynamic microphone, the vibrating diaphragm moves a coil of wire inside a permanent magnet, creating an electric current. The current varies according to the strength and frequency of the sound waves moving the diaphragm. Dynamic microphones are very rugged and can produce excellent sound. Most of the hand mikes used by news reporters are dynamic mikes. They're sometimes called moving coil microphones.

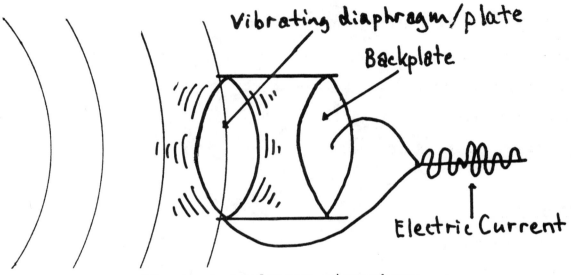

Electret condenser microphone

The diaphragm of an electret condenser microphone is actually one plate of a condenser, or capacitor. The diaphragm/plate and another plate hold an electric charge between them. As the diaphragm vibrates to sound waves, changing the distance between the two plates, a tiny electric current is created, varying according to the sound waves. A battery supplies power to amplify the signal to a usable level.

Because, unlike dynamic mikes, they don't contain heavy permanent magnets, condenser mikes can be made very small and lightweight. They can produce excellent sound. However, they do require batteries, which wear out and die. So carry backups.

Microphone pickup patterns.

A microphone's pickup pattern is the area in which it is most sensitive to incoming sound waves. There are two basic types of pickup patterns, omnidirectional and directional.

An omnidirectional mike picks up sound equally well from every direction. This is the most common pickup pattern; it looks like a sphere with the microphone at the center.

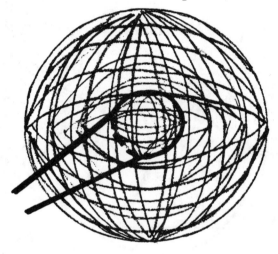

Omnidirectional pickup pattern

The two most common types of directional pickup patterns are the cardioid and the supercardioid, or shotgun.

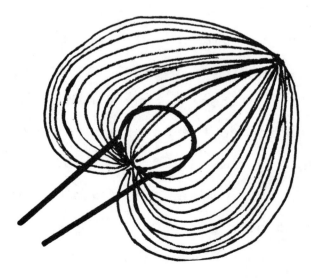

Cardioid pickup pattern

"Cardioid" comes from the Greek word meaning "heart-shaped." A cardioid pickup pattern looks like a heart, with the pointed end indicating the area of greatest sensitivity, directly in front of the microphone.

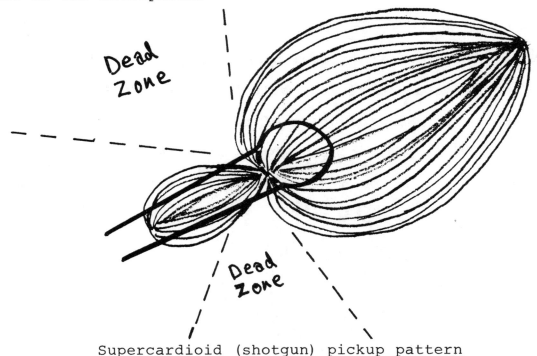

Supercardioid (shotgun) pickup pattern

The supercardioid mike is also called a shotgun mike; this is because the area of sensitivity is so narrow that, to pick up the correct sound, you have to aim the microphone like a shotgun directly at the source.

To eliminate or reduce unwanted sound hitting a directional microphone, angle the mike so the dead zone--the area of no sensitivity--is pointing at the unwanted sound. For example, tilting a supercardioid slightly upward, as pictured above, points the dead zone toward the floor, eliminating reflected sound from that direction.

Types of microphones

Film and video productions use three common types of microphones. From smallest to largest, they are the lavalier, the hand mike, and the shotgun.

The lavalier is a small, electret condenser mike, normally designed with an omnidirectional pickup pattern. (Some newer lavaliers have cardioid pickup patterns.) Lavalier mikes are designed to be worn on the chest of the speaker, either hung by a cord, or attached with a clip. Placed so close to the sound source--the speaker's mouth--they provide a very strong signal.

~HI!

Lavalier mikes record good sound because they are close to the source.

Sometimes you'll want to hide a lavalier mike under a tie or shirt. This presents two problems. First, any movement of clothing across or near the mike will be picked up; so use tape to hold the mike firmly in place, and don't hide it behind noisy materials, like silk. Secondly, anything you cover the mike with is going to block some of the incoming sound waves; so use porous, loose-knit material, like wool or cotton, that lets most of the sound through.

If you use a lavalier loose, off the chest, be aware that it will boost the higher frequencies, making voices sound shriller than normal. When a lavalier is worn on the chest, as it is designed to be, the boost compensates for the lack of high frequency voice tones under the chin.

The all-purpose <u>hand mike</u> is the most versatile and widely used in the industry. It can be either dynamic or condenser, with either an omnidirectional or a cardioid pickup pattern. With a stand, it can also be used as a desk or platform microphone.

Fishpole

<u>The all-purpose hand mike is the most versatile mike.</u>

The <u>supercardioid or shotgun mike</u> takes its name from its pickup pattern, discussed above. It's a great mike to use for distant sounds or in uncontrolled situations, like television news coverage. It's also very useful on a boom or fishpole in controlled situations, such as dramatic productions.

The great advantage of the shotgun mike--it's super-directionality--is also its greatest disadvantage. While it accepts sounds only within its narrow cone pickup pattern, it accepts <u>all</u> the sounds within that cone, in front of and behind your subject. A shotgun mike will pick up the voice of a man standing on the sidewalk across the street; unfortunately, it will also pick up the sound of cars passing in the foreground and the voices of people walking behind him.

<u>Shotgun mikes pick up everything</u>
<u>in the direction they're pointed.</u>

In responding to lower frequencies, below 250 or 300 Hz, the shotgun mike's pickup pattern is essentially cardioid. This means it picks up a lot of traffic noise, machine rumbles, and similar sounds. Most shotguns have a bass cutoff switch to filter out these frequencies.

Shotgun mikes are sensitive to sound echos--reverberation. If you use one in a "live" room--one with lots of echos--they'll only worsen the problem.

<u>Microphone selection</u>

Remember your viewer. Use the microphone that, under the circumstances, will best capture the sound you want your viewer to hear.

The surest way to get good clean sound from one person talking is to use a lavalier mike. Complications arise when you want to hide the mike: clothes rustle, muted sound. Multiple miking--putting lavs on several people at the same time--also complicates the procedure. When using several microphones, try to have only one microphone "open" or on at a time.

For a spur-of-the-moment walking street interview with a politician, an omnidirectional hand mike is best--not because it gives the best sound, but because it gives the best sound under the circumstances. It's almost impossible to not record something usable with an omnidirectional hand mike.

For uncontrolled documentary shooting, a shotgun is the microphone of choice. With it, you can record understandable, usable sound at any distance, from an inch to infinity. The sound may not always be perfect, but you'll have something to work with.

The shotgun, used on a boom--an extendable arm-like microphone holder--can provide excellent sound for rehearsed, dramatic programs--or any other circumstance where a number of people are talking from known positions. The shotgun's pickup pattern is so narrow that exact aiming is absolutely essential.

If I could have only one mike for all situations, I'd choose a dynamic hand mike with a cardioid pickup pattern. Dynamic for durability. Cardioid for the pickup pattern--selective but not too selective; you can be a little off in aiming and still cover the sound source. This mike works well as a hand mike, as a desk mike, and as a boom or fishpole mike.

74

Sound waves bounce.

From the source, spherical sound waves travel straight out in all directions. When they hit a hard, non-porous surface, they bounce--like waves hitting the edge of a swimming pool.

Since sound waves bounce, you can bounce or reflect unwanted sounds away from your microphone. The most typical example is to position a subject's body between the unwanted sound and the microphone. Other objects, like sun reflectors, work just as well.

You can bounce unwanted sound waves away from your mike.

A surface composed of many smaller surfaces facing different directions is said to be porous. When sound waves hit a porous surface, they bounce back and forth, getting smaller and smaller, in the same way pond waves disperse when they flow into a patch of reeds. Foam rubber, like that used in microphone windscreens, and thick felt are good examples of porous surfaces. Extremely porous surfaces, which completely eliminate sound waves, are said to be sound absorbent.

Sounds in any enclosed space, like a room, are reflected back and forth many times, getting progressively smaller and quieter as they die away, or decay. The total effect of the reflected sound waves is called <u>reverberation</u>. If a room is dead, with no reverberation, sounds die quickly, with no decay; they seem muffled and dull. In a well-designed sound studio, with good reverberation, sounds decay smoothly and quickly. A room with too much reverberation produces echos--repetitions of the original sound.

A dead room can be livened up by adding hard reflective surfaces--tables, plastic screens, pieces of glass--and removing porous items, like upholstered furniture. If you can't remove the furniture, cover it with slick plastic sheets.

Excessive reverberation, or echo, can be muted by filling the room with many different surfaces--furniture, boxes, people-- at different angles to each other. Cover hard surfaces with porous materials. Put carpet on the floor.

Sound perspective.

Perspective is the way things seem from a particular point of view. It's relative; it depends on where you are. From the perspective of an ant, a child is a giant. From the perspective of a tall building, the child is an ant.

In film and video, perspective is based on the viewer. The camera can give the viewer the perspective of an ant, a child, or a building. Sound perspective is how close what the viewer hears matches what he sees.

Think about the last time someone shouted to you from across the street. In addition to his voice, you also heard a lot of ambient sounds--sounds from the surrounding area--like traffic, wind, birds, airplanes, radios, people talking. Your caller's voice probably sounded thin, not robust, with perhaps a little reverberation. This didn't bother you, because you could <u>see</u> he was across the street; the sound of his voice matched what your eyes told you to expect. Distant sound perspective matched distant visual perspective.

Now imagine that same person walking across the street, going inside your house, sitting down in your living room, and talking to you. In these circumstances, his words sound clearer, there is less ambient sound, and you hear the full richness of his voice. This seems natural to you, since just as his across-the-street voice matched what you saw then, so his across-the-living-room voice matches what you see now. Close sound perspective matches close visual perspective.

But how would you react to hearing an across-the-street voice coming out of a person sitting in your living room? It would sound a little strange, wouldn't it? What if your friend shouted from across the street and he sounded as if he were a few feet away in your living room? The sound perspective would not match the visual perspective. You would feel as if your eyes were in one place and your ears somewhere else.

In the same way, drastic mismatches of visual and sound perspectives in a film or video distract the viewer; they pull him out of the world you are creating and divert him from your message.

To get correct sound perspective in film and video, the easiest way is to place the microphone in the same position as the camera; then sound and picture have the same perspective. However, this is not always possible or even desirable.

Say you have a wide shot of a young couple walking down the beach, talking. The camera is sixty feet away. With the microphone at the camera, you'll be able to record their voices with the proper sound perspective; but you'll also record a lot of wind and wave noise. In fact, the ambient noise may be so high that you won't be able to understand them.

Still, let's assume you can record legible sound of your young lovers from sixty feet away. Then you move the camera in for closeups; the microphone moves with you. Now the voices you record will be clearer, richer, and with less wind and wave noise. The sound will again match the picture. You have the shots you need for editing.

In editing, when you cut from the wide shot to the close shot, there will be a drastic change in the quality of the voices, plus a noticeable drop in wind and wave noise. While totally realistic, the change in sound quality may distract your viewer, especially if you cut back and forth between the shots.

In the mix, there's little you can do to make the thin wide shot voices sound as good as the richer close shot voices. So, to smooth the transitions between the two shots, you must make the close voices sound more like the wide voices. You can do this by adding more wave and wind noise to the closeups, and by cutting some frequencies out of the closeup voices to make them sound thinner. In other words, take your good sound and make it as bad as your bad sound. With all respect to professional soundpersons, I prefer to work differently. I record the separate elements that make up sound perspective as cleanly and directly as possible, then create the proper sound perspective in the mix.

Sound perspective consists of direct sound, ambient sound, and reflected sound. Close sound perspective consists mostly of strong direct sound, with lesser amounts of ambient and reflected (reverberated) sound mixed in. Distant sound perspective contains less and weaker direct sound, with more ambient and reflected sound mixed in.

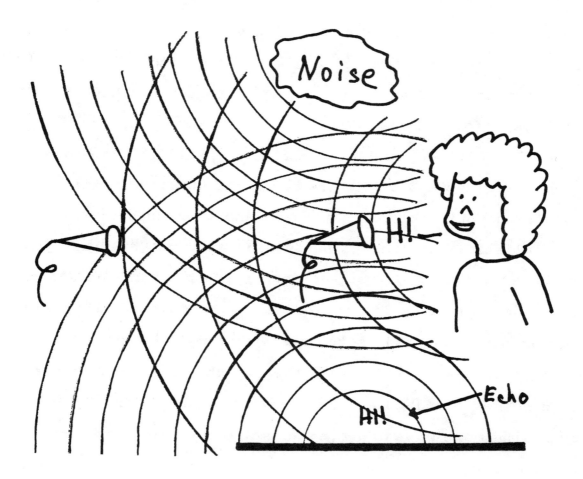

Close sound perspective consists mostly of direct sound. Distant sound perspective contains more ambient and reflected sound.

For my main sound track, which is usually voices, I record the cleanest, most consistent, understandable sound possible. For the beach sequence, I would use lavaliers on the actors in every scene. I record background noise, or presence, separately.

In the mix, I simulate the wide shot perspective by raising the volume of the backgound track and slightly lowering the volume of the voice track. If it seems necessary, I cut some frequencies from the wide shot voices to make them sound thinner. I might also add a little artificial reverberation. I reverse the procedure for closeup perspective.

Working this way, with two separate tracks, I have much more control over the sound I present to my viewer; if I want, I can deliberately sacrifice correct perspective in order to make my main voices more understandable or less understandable.

If you aren't going to mix your program, I recommend that you forget about perspective and concentrate on legibility. It's much more important that your viewer understand your message. If your program is good in all other respects, the average viewer will never notice whether the sound perspective is correct or not. The proof of this is in 90% of everything you see on television and at the movies. Part or all of the dialogue, and usually all of the sound effects, are recorded separately and cleanly and with close mikes, then mixed in.

Record clean sound.

As a general rule, record your sound as closely and as cleanly as possible, with the broadest possible frequency range. Resist the temptation to filter or modify the frequency response

of the sound as it is recorded.   You can always cut frequencies
later, but you can't add them when you never recorded them in the
first place.   One exception: bass cut-off filters on shotgun
mikes to eliminate traffic noise and other low-frequency noise.

When recording on videotape, you'll record cleaner, richer
sound if you use a separate audio recorder that is synchronized
to your video recorder. Audio tape has more room for the sound
track and can thus record a wider range of frequencies and volume
levels.   Also, the recording technology used in dedicated audio
recorders is usually better.

If at all possible, use the same microphone or the same type
of microphone to record all of an actor's lines, no matter when
or where you record them.   The difference in sound quality from
one type of mike to another can be noticeable and distracting.

Just as a good monitor is important for judging your images,
so a good pair of isolating headphones with a broad frequency
response is important to judge your sound.   Isolating headphones
completely surround the ears and let you hear only what you are
recording.

When deciding how to frame a shot, consider not only the
visual elements, but also sound.   Sometimes a slight change of
camera angle can greatly reduce a wind or noise problem.   Moving
a prop or piece of furniture can make it possible to get a mike
closer to an actor.   Modifying the route an actor walks through
the set can make it easier to follow him with a boom mike.

Whenever there is a noticeable sound effect in a scene, such
as a car starting, a door slamming, a machine running in the
background, take a few extra seconds to record the same sound

close, without picture. These effects are called <u>wild effects</u>, different from <u>sync effects</u>, which are recorded at the same time as the picture. Wild effects can substitute for sync effects that are low or muddled. They also add depth and continuity to your picture; unrelated shots of workers come alive and tie together when you add appropriate sound effects and background noise. Closeup wild effects stand out; they add texture to your program. And, since they are clean and isolated, you can control them completely in the mix. As with pictures, you'll do yourself and your editor a big favor if you slate all your wild effects, either by voice or--on video--visually.

You can do lots of things outside the camera frame to improve the quality of your sound. Put carpet on the floor. Hang blankets to reduce reflected sound. Use extra people as human windbreaks. If background and screen direction match, you can move an actor to a different, quieter area for the closeups.

When recording sound around professional movie and television lights, don't let your mike cords run parallel and close to electrical cables--it will put a hum on your sound track. If you must lay a mike cord across an electrical cable, lay it at right angles; better still, raise it up on a bridge made from a box, a stool or a chair.

Most sound recorders have a button to generate a 1000 Hz tone. Record thirty to sixty seconds of tone at the beginning of each new reel or cassette. On videotape, record tone at the same time as you record your color bars. The sound engineer will use the 1000 Hz tone to calibrate his equipment for best reproduction of your original sound.

Recording voices and presence

Syncsound is sound recorded in synchronization with the camera, such as a person talking on camera. Voice-over is a narrative voice heard over the picture but not seen. When the same person is heard in syncsound and voice-over, try to record all the lines with the same mike and in the same place, so the quality of the voice will be consistent in the final program. If the syncsound is recorded in a noisy location, record the voice-over at the same time, in a place nearby that's quieter. If that's not possible, record the voice-over at the same time of day as you recorded the syncsound. People's voices change noticeably over the course of a day; the same voice recorded in morning and afternoon can sound like two different people.

Presence, or ambience, is the sound of a location without any single sound predominating. For example, factory presence would be the muddle of different sounds you'd hear standing in the middle of the assembly line. Lonely beach presence would be wind, waves and bird noises.

If you're recording dialogue, presence is the sound between the words. Whenever you finish recording dialogue at a location, leave the recorder set at the same level, tell everybody to hold still, and record thirty seconds of presence. This serves several purposes in the mix.

First, presence serves as an audio bridge to ease the transition when you cut from one location to another, or from syncsound to voice-over. Fade in extra presence before a cut, then fade it out afterward. This will smooth out sudden changes or cutoffs of background presence.

Presence can be used to fill the holes when you space out narration. You may think a studio recording is perfectly quiet, but lengthen a narrator's pause by a few seconds and leave the pause completely noiseless; you'll notice it. You need the recording booth's presence to fill the space.

A presence recording helps in the cleaning up of sound tracks. Voice tracks recorded with air conditioner hum in the background are a common problem. Playing a continuous loop of the presence recording, the sound engineer can use an equalizer to selectively boost or decrease selected frequencies until he finds the air conditioner frequencies and lowers or eliminates them. He can then process the voice track through the same equalizer settings, cleaning the track of the air conditioner noise.

Voice-slate and keep a sound log

If you record double-system sound, with a separate audio recorder, voice-slate everything you record. A voice-slate is a recorded description; without it, you have to guess what's on the tape. For syncsound, the traditional clapstick slate provides both a voice-slate ("Scene one, Take one!") and a common audio-visual sync point when the clapstick closes (CLAAAK!).

Keep a sound log, listing everything you've recorded, in the order you recorded it. This will help you quickly locate recorded material later, for use in editing. When shooting single-system videotape, you can either combine your sound log with your camera log, or keep a separate sound log, depending on the needs of the production.

As with the camera log, the sound log includes as little or as much information as you want to put on it. I recommend noting at least the scene and take number, the mike and recorder used, the location, videotape time code if applicable, and a description of the sound recorded. Circle the numbers of the good takes.

If your audio tape doesn't have time code, with an exact address for each take, separate your sound takes with 1000 Hz beep tone. At the end of each sound take, hit the tone generator button for two quick beeps and a long one: Beep Beep Beeeeeeeep. Later, to quickly locate a particular take on the sound log, highspeed through the tape, counting the easily recognized three-beep sequences till you get to the one you want.

Remember your viewer.

The purpose of your program is to get your viewer to react in a certain way. Keep this in mind when deciding what sounds to record and how. If you want to communicate a positive feeling about an industry, record people talking in quiet areas; if you want to make your viewer uncomfortable, record workers shouting to be heard over a clamorous assembly line. If you need to present the assembly line in a positive way, show it with the sound mixed low under an off-camera narrator's voice; or consider dubbing the assembly line worker's voices. In the same way, you can make an office seem more chaotic by adding extra background telephones, typewriters and voices in the mix.

When in doubt, record voice, sound effects and presence separately and cleanly. This will give you maximum flexibility in your mix.

7. Editing

The human eye as editor

The eye "edits" automatically by focusing on what interests it. Let's go for an imaginary drive. First we see a medium wide shot ahead of the road. Then we "cut" to a close-up of the speedometer and gauges. A quick medium shot to the right as we glance at our passenger. A zoom-in to a warning sign coming up. Get the idea? We see in terms of basic sequences.

The basic shot our eyes give us has an angle of view approximately 25 degrees wide. This is equivalent to about a 50mm lens on 35mm film, or a 25mm lens on either 16mm film, 2/3" video tubes, or CCD's. Through sideways peripheral vision, we can sense movement outside the 25 degree area but still not visualize clearly what's there.

Here's an experiment to demonstrate the principles of editing. Find a room that has lots of visual interest--lots of things in it. Ask a friend to stand as far from you as possible while reading the next section aloud. Face your friend and follow the instructions exactly.

[BEGIN EXPERIMENT- YOUR FRIEND SHOULD READ THE FOLLOWING ALOUD]

"Look straight ahead and try to see as much of me and the room as you can. This is your establishing shot. Notice that as you change your area of interest, without moving your head, you can shift first to a medium shot of me from the waist up, then to a close-up of my face.

"As I slowly walk to my right, zoom back to a wider shot. Now, without moving your head, shift your eyes right for a

cutaway of something else in the room. You can do all this
comfortably.

"When I say 'GO,' move your whole head quickly to the left
and look at what's there. GO! When I say 'GO,' move your head
quickly to the right and notice what's there. GO!

"Each time you move your head quickly, you should feel a
moment of softness, of perceptive hesitation, as your brain
rushes to drink in the new visual information and absorb it. The
fast image change makes your brain play catch-up.

"Now, when I say 'GO,' move your head <u>slowly</u> to the left and
look at what's there. GO!

"When I say 'GO!,' move your head <u>slowly</u> to the right and
look at what's there. GO!

"When you move your head slowly, the new visual information
is introduced gradually. Your brain has time to absorb it as it
is introduced. When you finally get turned sideways, the image
is complete in your mind.

"When I say 'GO,' cover your ears with your hands, count to
three slowly; then remove your hands. GO!

"Now close your eyes. Without opening your eyes, move your
head to your right. Look down. Now, open and close your eyes as
fast as you can. What did you see? Now open your eyes and leave
them open. Do you see anything now that you missed before?

"One last experiment. Look at your watch. Now, without
moving your head, move your wrist up and down rapidly and try to
read the watch label. Now hold the watch still and read the
time."

[END OF EXPERIMENT]

This is the essence of editing. In the experiment your friend <u>controlled</u> what you saw and heard. He "edited" your reality. As a film or video editor, you edit the reality of your viewer--you control the window through which he sees and hears the world of your program. Your choices of pictures and sounds determine how well your message gets across, and how the viewer reacts to it. The principles demonstrated in our experiment are the basic principles of editing.

To communicate clearly and tension-free, don't surprise the viewer. Use an establishing shot to show the viewer where everything is. Keep the camera still unless there's a reason to move it. Remember how easy it was to focus on wide shots, medium shots and closeups of your friend without moving your head?

Give the viewer new images and sounds slowly enough for his brain to absorb them. If possible, lead into camera moves by following a known object moving within the frame, such as your friend walking across the room in our experiment above. Use camera moves that <u>ease</u> in and <u>ease</u> out--remember the difference between moving your head fast and moving it slow?

If you present totally new information, give the viewer a little extra time to absorb it and feel comfortable with it. Remember opening your eyes for just a fraction of a second, then holding them open longer? You needed that extra time to absorb the new information.

In some circumstances, particularly dramatic programs, you <u>want</u> to send a muddled message, or create tension in your viewer. You want to make the style itself part of your message. To do this, you deliberately surprise him. You push unfamiliar images

and sounds on him faster than his brain can absorb them. You cut
to new scenes without clear establishing shots. You cut quickly
from one shot to another. You make fast, jerky camera moves.
You use unsteady camera frames, blurred images, indistinct or
distorted sound. These are all valid techniques, as long as they
are intentional, and not simply bad work on your part.

Read the script. Divorce the director.

Beginning editors want to jump right into cutting. This is
a mistake. First, read your script and make sure you understand
perfectly how the viewer is supposed to react to the program.
Base all your editing decisions on the question, "Is this the
best way to make the viewer react the way I want him to?" As you
work, visualize the viewer watching each cut.

Start the editing process by divorcing yourself from the
person who directed the program, even if the person is you.
Think of him or her as some stranger whose ideas and shots you
will judge strictly on their own merit. Look at the script and
the pictures and sound as if you'd never seen them before. It
helps if you can schedule the end of shooting and the beginning
of editing a few weeks apart.

I've seen many programs weakened in the editing because a
director was personally attached to a concept, a shot, or a
sequence that simply didn't work on the screen. This usually
happens when the director can't separate the idea or the shot
from the attached memories.

Remember all those ideas you, as director, had about how
certain scenes would be edited together? Remember how you stayed

up late working out concepts in your head, then overslept and missed breakfast? Forget everything except the ideas. Consider them fresh, as if someone else had thought of them. Then, if they don't work, throw them out. So you lost some sleep and missed breakfast; what has that got to do with getting your viewer to react in a certain way? Nothing. It's excess baggage; throw it out.

Remember how much trouble you had getting that one incredibly beautiful shot? Look at it now as simply a shot that either works or doesn't work toward your program's goals. The viewer doesn't care how much trouble you had getting the camera into position and waiting for just the right light; he doesn't care that it took you two months to get permission to film at that location. That's all off-screen; all that matters is what the viewer sees on the screen, in the window that you control. If a shot doesn't work there--if it doesn't move the viewer the way it's supposed to--toss it.

Make sure you have all the materials before you start

Faced with a large jumble of building materials and told to build a house, your first step would probably be to organize the supplies--stack all the lumber in one place, the bricks in another, and so on. You could then check your stacks against the building plans to make sure you have all the materials called for. If there are no plans, you could make a list of what's in the stacks, then design your own house based on what you've got to work with.

Editing a program is like building a house. The director supplies you with a jumble of raw material. You organize it, then see if you have everything the script calls for. If you don't have a script, camera log or sound log, you make a list--called an editing log--of the pictures and sound you have, then construct a program from the available materials.

Organizing the material is a two-step operation. First, you separate out all the good material, then you arrange it in script order. The good and no good (NG) takes should already be marked on script notes, assistant cameraperson's notes, or the soundperson's notes. If you have no notes, then the director should indicate to you which shots to throw away and which to keep.

By working only with usable material, arranged in order, you spend more of your editing time actually editing. The alternative is to continually jump back and forth over unrelated and unusable shots, switching reels or cassettes, as you put the program together. This is not only time-consuming but distracting.

To organize film workprint, spool your good takes off on separate labeled cores or, if they're short, hang them on numbered pins in a trim bin. Leave the bad stuff on the original reels. After you've gone through everything, resplice all the good shots, in script order, onto master editing reels. Then you're ready to edit.

With linear videotape editing systems, the edited tape copy is matched back to the original material by referring to the original tape's time code--which identifies each frame by hour, minute, second and frame. If you shoot videotape without time code, and you can't add time code later, then you have to edit from your original unorganized material. The only way to make this task easier is to to shoot all the scenes for each section, no matter when or where they're shot, on the same cassette or reel. That way, your recorded material is close to the final script order to begin with.

To organize a time coded linear videotape edit, first make a work dub or copy with your original time code visibly reproduced on the screen (a window dub). While it's not practical to separate individual takes, as with film, you can divide your program into ten or more sections, then copy the best takes of each section onto their own cassette. If you want, you can then go down one more generation and organize the scenes in exact script order. (An alternative is to do what I suggested above for shooting without time code--shoot all related shots on the same reel or cassette, effectively pre-organizing your material.)

To organize a non-linear, computer-based video edit, the most important thing is to log all material with as much detail as possible, either in the field with a logger program or as you digitize onto your hard drive. In your descriptions, use consistent key words, like identifying every scene as "Scene #_". Use the same abbreviations, like "MS," "LS," etc. Try to use the same descriptive terms, like "good" to describe usable takes and "NG" for no good takes. If you have a script, use key words from the script in your log descriptions.

When you start to edit, use your video editing program's search function to search for "Scene #23, Joe, MS, good" and you'll call up only clips whose log entries contain those words.

If you must edit without first organizing your material, I suggest you spend as much time as possible viewing and reviewing before you start cutting. The better you know your pictures and sound, the more effectively you'll be able to edit them. Whenever possible, note exact reel and time code numbers of your best takes.

Unscripted sequences and programs are the most fun to edit, because they're actually written in the editing. As you view the material, make a detailed log (or add your own notes to a <u>copy</u> of the camera/sound log). Look for your most powerful pictures and sounds--save them for the beginning and end of your program and to liven up the middle. Look for connections between scenes-- similar colors, moves, sounds, dialogue. Then do a <u>paper edit</u>.

A paper edit is a script constructed from cut-up sections of an editing log. You arrange and rearrange your material until it works as a script. Think of yourself as a scriptwriter who is reconstructing a wonderful script that somehow got cut into pieces and mixed up. Use all the techniques of style and shape and texture that a scriptwriter would use. Design a program that makes the viewer react the way you want him to. Then tape together all the sections in their new order and proceed to edit, using the paper edit as you would a formal script. A good paper edit makes it possible for a documentary to move the viewer as well or better than the most tightly scripted program. A computer word processor, or better still an outline or idea processor, makes the task easier.

Please, PLEASE don't make the mistake of editing a documentary or other unscripted program without a good log and a paper edit. You will waste a lot of time and probably find yourself at two o'clock in the morning with five minutes remaining in the program and no material left to fill it with. That's the beauty of a paper edit; it lets you make the most of what you've got.

Establish your program's world; then re-establish it.

The editor's first priority is to establish the world of the program for the viewer, to introduce him to this new reality and make him comfortable in it. If the viewer is wondering where he is, he's not thinking about your message. Show him an establishing shot within the first few shots of a sequence.

Narration or dialogue can serve just as well as a visual to let the viewer know where he is: "As we look through a high-powered microscope, we can see the sperm..."

Previous, related shots can help establish a new location: after several sequences about biological labs, the viewer will assume that a white-coated person shown in medium close-up is another lab person, even without another wide shot of a lab.

If the viewer is already familiar with the subject, he can figure out where he is based on less information from you. For example, a program for mechanics on carburetor rebuilding can begin with the carburetor already out of the car; you can assume your mechanic/viewer will know immediately what a carburetor is and where it came from.

After you establish, re-establish frequently. Editing is a sequential process, one scene after the other, always moving forward. Most people can't remember the visuals of more than two

or three scenes back. A series of closeups, with no visual
reminders of screen geography, can disorient the viewer and suck
him into a perceptional tunnel; he'll spend more time trying to
figure out where he is than paying attention to what you're
telling him. So, cut back to a wider shot from time to time to
remind the viewer where everything is. This will keep his feet
on the ground and his attention on the contents of your program.

Look for basic sequences, then use them.

If the director shot basic sequences, use them. A basic
sequence, cutting back and forth between related shots in the
same location, mimics the way the viewer sees life around him
every day. It communicates information better than a series of
unrelated scenes, each coming as a surprise to the viewer.

If no basic sequences were shot, look for pictures and
sounds that can be edited together in the form of basic
sequences. For example, a series of interviews with teachers at
a school, all shot in similar locations with similar camera
framings, and with no cutaways. Rather than cut from one head-
and-shoulders shot to the next, find cutaways to put between
them. Let's say Teacher #1 talks about science classes, while
Teacher #2 talks about student discipline. Finish Teacher #1's
comments off-camera over a shot of students working in a lab.
Start Teacher #2's comments over the same shot, then continue
with Teacher #2 on camera. The shot of the students is a natural
cutaway for both interviews, as well as a natural link. The
final effect is of one continuous interview with a cutaway,
rather than two separate talking heads.

The Great Underlying Rule of Editing:

<u>Make sure each new shot is different.</u>

Imagine yourself at a wedding reception, moving down a receiving line that's so crowded you can just barely see the person in front of you. After being introduced to a man and shaking his hand, you move down one person--and meet the same man again! Well, actually it's his identical twin. When you meet the second twin, you do a double take. Why? Because you were expecting each person in line to look different. In your momentary confusion, you have to ask the second twin to repeat his name. The same phenomenon applies to editing.

Each time you cut to a new shot, the viewer expects to see something different. If the new shot is very similar to the old shot, the viewer is momentarily confused and his attention is jarred away from your program's content. Therefore, each new shot should be clearly different in content, framing, or both, from the previous shot. The elements of a basic sequence--wide shot, medium shot, closeup, and cutaway--while similar in content, must be clearly different in framing and camera angle or they won't cut together smoothly.

Pacing - how fast things change

Pacing is the rate at which you change your pictures and sounds. A good editor gently leads the viewer from shot to shot without distracting him from the program's content. If the content of your program is totally interesting to the viewer, do nothing; no one got bored looking at that single camera shot of the first men on the moon. There are only two reasons to change your pictures and sounds: to better tell your message, or to keep the viewer's interest. Never cut just to be cutting. Right now, you're reading this book; if the rest of the pages were blank, or a naked person walked by, you'd switch your attention away from the book. Editing works the same way. The general rule is to stay with a shot as long as it's effective in telling the message or keeping the viewer interested, then cut to something new. To know when to cut, you have to know your viewer and how you want him to react.

A good editor anticipates his viewer. Before he can begin to drift away, the editor shows him a new reason for staying. The editor does a dance with the viewer's attention, giving a gentle tug from time to time to keep him in step with the program.

To give something importance, show it longer. This is the visual equivalent of drawing out a phrase in conversation. For example, "a hundred dollars" said quickly is peanuts; but "A HUHHHHHHNDRED DAWWWWWWWWWWLARS" is a lot of money. A sequence about breast cancer will have more impact if you linger a beat or two on a closeup of a prosthesis, rather than skip quickly past.

To give something importance, show it more often.   Repetition works. How well would you know your multiplication tables if you hadn't repeated them umpteen times? Show a safety technique one time, and the viewer might remember it. Show it a second or third time, in slightly different ways, and he will remember it better.

If you're presenting new or complicated information, cut slower; give the viewer more time to absorb your message. If you cut to a new scene before the viewer totally understands what's on the screen at the moment, you'll frustrate him. For example, an introductory film on any subject should be more slowly paced than an intermediate film on the same subject; the intermediate information will already be somewhat familiar to the viewer.

Most viewers are accustomed to seeing a dissolve or a full-screen wipe used to indicate a change in time, place, or subject matter. If you use these visual effects for any other purpose, or if you use them excessively, however, they call attention away from your program's message. The exception is when these and other visual effects are used in montages, commercials, music videos, and television news and sports. In these instances visual effects are meant to call attention to themselves; they're part of the message. Used for that purpose, they're very effective.

Use an editing style consistent with the program's goals.

Style, you'll recall, is the way you deliver your message, as opposed to content, which is the message itself. Your editing style is determined by which pictures and sounds you select, the order in which you present them to your viewer, and how fast you change from one picture or sound to the next--pacing.

Your editing style should complement the style already established by your script, the director, and the cameraperson. If your program is well-written, well-directed, and well-shot, follow the editing rules I've discussed: establish and re-establish, use basic sequences, make every new shot different, and match your pacing to the viewer's interest. If you do this, your editing style will be invisible and your viewer will get your program's message loud and clear.

If the material you're given to edit is less than perfect, you can make it work better by breaking the rules and increasing tension--giving the viewer a nudge from time to time to keep him alert and interested. This is a delicate operation.

To increase tension, cut faster than expected, use unusually framed shots, cut to unexpected shots, use jump cuts. A jump cut is when you cut from a wide shot of a man with his arm up to a closeup of the same man with his arm down; on the scene change, the arm "jumps" down. This is also called bad continuity.

Try to synchronize the amount of tension you inject with the rising and falling of your viewer's interest. You might precede a sequence of unavoidably dull instruction with a sequence cut progressively quicker, to subtly stimulate the viewer. Or you could raise the background music level at the beginning of the dull sequence to make the viewer strain slightly to understand the narrator, thus involuntarily paying more attention.

There is a limit, however, to what the editor can do to make a program work. If the writing, directing and camerawork are bad, no amount of editing tricks can save it. You can't make a a gourmet meal from garbage, nor can you edit a good program from poor material.

If your editing style is supposed to be noticeable, if it's supposed to intentionally form part of your message, then break the rules. But first be sure your viewer is going to react the way you want him to. With the exception of montages, which I'll discuss later in this chapter, the best editing style is usually transparent.

Sound in Editing

Sound is an excellent connecting device across cuts. L-cuts are particularly useful in dialogue scenes and for linking documentary elements together. They are the basic technique for interweaving pictures and sounds to add texture.

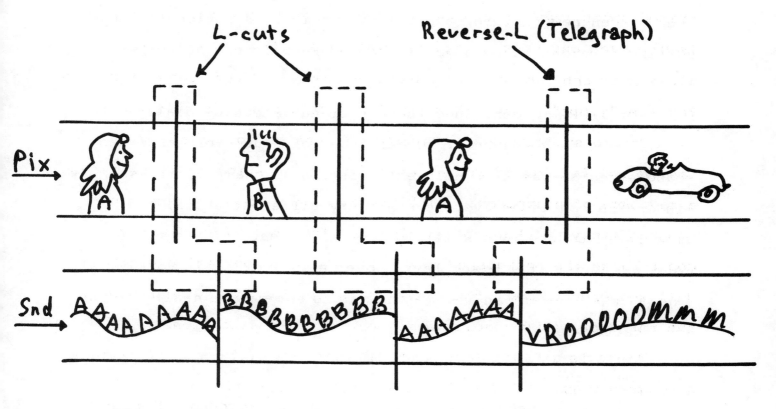

If Person A is talking to Person B, cut to the picture of B listening to the last of A's dialogue, then B begins to talk. Just before B finishes, cut to picture of A listening, then A begins to talk. These are L-Cuts.

L-Cuts give your program texture and forward movement. First, they tease the viewer with a picture that doesn't match the sound he's hearing; then they immediately satisfy his curiosity, drawing him into the next scene.

When B interrupts A, use a Reverse-L cut. Cut to B's sound while still seeing A's picture, then cut to B's picture.

The Reverse-L is also called a telegraph cut, because it gives the viewer an early hint of what's to come. It smoothes an edit by cutting first to the incoming scene's sound, then later to the new picture. I use Reverse-L's to bring in the backgound sound or music of a new scene early. By first cutting in new sound, then new picture, the transition is less noticeable than cutting straight to both new sound and new picture at the same time.

I've already mentioned the use of narration or dialogue to help establish a sequence. Other types of sound--presence and sound effects--can also help establish. For example, if assembly line noise continues over several very different shots, the viewer can assume he's still in the same area. If the noise continues, but at a lower level, over a shot of a man working at a desk, the viewer can assume the man is somewhere nearby in the same factory.

Background music.

Most music used in editing is in the background. Like other aspects of editing, background music is most effective when it is neither noticed nor remembered by the viewer. Nonetheless, it plays a very important role.

Background music can help to convey a mood or to reinforce your program's message. The viewer will associate his feelings about the music with what he's seeing on the screen. For example, when demonstrating safe work procedures, use upbeat and positive music. When demonstrating bad work habits, use

strident, even discordant music, to reinforce your negative
narrative and visual message.

Background music can give forward momentum to your program.
Dull pictures and narration can come alive when coupled with an
optimistic, peppy piece of music.

Background music can give cohesion and order to your
program. When the same piece of music covers a series of
unrelated shots, the viewer knows instinctively that they have
something in common and adjusts his frame of mind accordingly.

Selecting and cutting library music.

Background music is like plumbing: its function is more
important than its beauty. To function properly, background
music must be consistent in theme and volume, and it must stay in
the background. Most commercial music has too many variations--
too many noticeable peaks and valleys--to serve as background
music. Your best bet is library music--music specially composed
for use in film and television programs.

There are thousands of pieces of excellent library music
available. Most editing houses have at least one collection on
hand. The license fee you pay is usually less than the cost of
commercial music rights, and much less than original music.

When searching library music, keep your mind open; often a
selection you listen to for one purpose will actually work better
somewhere else in the program. The most important thing is to
find music that conveys the mood of your program and that doesn't
clash with your voice track. Try to find pieces of music that
all have similar instrumentation and style, especially when one

selection is going to pick up immediately after another ends. If
the selections will be separated in the final program, this isn't
as important.

Many pieces of library music begin and end with musically
neutral percussion sections; this makes transitions easier.
Also, a strong sound effect or piece of dialogue can blanket a
musical change and make it less noticeable. Or you can do a
musical dissolve in the mix, fading the old music out while
fading the new music in. This is called a segue, pronounced SAY-
gway.

There are three ways to edit a piece of library music into
your program sound tracks. You can head-sync it, starting the
music where the picture section starts, then fade the music out
at the end of the section. You can tail-sync the music, lining
it up so it ends when the picture section ends, then fade it in
at the beginning of the section. Or you can cut the music
selection in the middle, head-sync the front half on one track,
tail-sync the second half on another track, and do a segue or a
cut where they cross.

If you have the budget for original music, plan for it the
same way you would plan to select library music; write out all
your requirements as clearly as possible, and show the composer
the edited program. Sometimes it helps the composer if you show
him some library or commercial music that is similar to what you
want. Most importantly, don't let the composer get carried away
and create background music that pushes out and calls attention
to itself when it shouldn't.

Sound mixing - separate your tracks.

You go into a sound mix with two objectives: 1) to improve the quality and effectiveness of your original sound recordings; and 2) to mix all your sound elements--voice, music and sound effects--together in such a way that they help get your message across to the viewer. Both objectives are best served by separating your sound elements off onto as many separate audio tracks as possible.

By having a sound element on its own separate track, you have maximum control over it. If, in the recording of a conversation, Person A talks very loud and Person B talks very softly, the sound mixer will be continually adjusting the volume up and down during the mix to maintain a consistent sound level. However, if Person A's voice is put on one track and Person B's on another, then the sound mixer can set a separate volume level for each track and leave it there. He can also equalize or modify the frequency response of Person A's voice without affecting Person B.

Create a separate sound track for each sound element or group of similar elements. For example, if your original recordings are good and you don't plan to modify them extensively in the mix, you might put all the principal men's voices on one track, all the principal women's voices on another, and all the supporting, less important voices on a third track. If a particular voice is going to be extensively modified in the mix, put it on a separate track, or on a track where it is well separated in time from other elements on the same track--time the mixer will need to adjust his settings.

Mixing cues tell the mixer what's on each track, when it occurs, and what you want done with it. Normally they're prepared on mixing cue sheets, with the film footage or running time or timecode indicated for each event. I use a vertical line to indicate the length of the sound, a horizontal dash to indicate the beginning or end of a sound, an upside-down V to indicate a fade-in, and a large V to mark a fade-out. Feel free to use any other symbol that works for you and your mixer.

Don't worry about drawing mix cues that are exact graphic representations of time, such as making each vertical inch equal ten seconds. If you need a whole page to clearly show everything that's happening in ten seconds, then use the whole page. If nothing happens for three minutes except the same voice and the same music, represent the whole section in a couple of inches. Your mix cues are a tool to make your job easier; don't become a slave to them.

Sometimes, for simpler mixes, I mark my mix cues directly on a clean copy of the script. Since most of the cues are tied to either visuals or dialogue, the script/mix cues format is easier for the mixer to follow than a traditional chart with numbers only. I still put in numbers where I need them, however. To make the cues stand out from the script, I use a different colored ink, like red, or green.

On the following two pages are examples of a traditional mix cues chart and a script marked with mix cues. This script happens to be in dramatic format, but you can mark up a two-column script just as easily.

VOICE 1	VOICE 2	MUS	EFX

00 ——————————— START ———————————

9 BEEP

22 F1

ESL 1020-B2
"FOGGY
NIGHT

45 DOOR

25 ⌐ "HI...

92 ⌐ ...BYE" 92 ⌐ "JOE... 92 FO

101 ⌐ FOOT
120 ⌐ STEPS

↓ CONT

Traditional mix cues chart:

VOICE 1	VOICE 2	MUS	EFX

32. INTERIOR - DAY - LIVING ROOM

JASON is asleep on the couch. SARAH enters   **190 DOOR**
quickly from the sun porch, slamming the door,
then stops abruptly when she sees JASON.

                    JASON
                 (half asleep)
Huh? Whuzzat?   **202   F1**

                    SARAH
Sorry, I wasn't aware there
was anyone in here.   **TM 1001
                                         B-16
                    JASON   "JUNKY"**
Thassalright. Iwuz jus
leavin...

JASON tries to stand up, then falls back
down on the couch. SARAH turns away in
disgust.

                    SARAH
Didn't you promise Mother
you'd stop drinking? You sot!
You disgusting, reprehensible
drunk!

JASON finally sits up.

                    JASON
Thass one way of puttin it,
I s'ppose.

SARAH walks over and looms over him.

                    SARAH
How could you? How could you?
Don't you care about anybody
but yourself?

JASON holds his head in his hands. He sighs
deeply.

                    JASON
Uh, uh, uh...

He falls back on the couch, unconscious.   **235 DOOR**
Disgusted, SARAH walks back out onto the
sun porch, slamming the door behind her.

                                         ↓CONT

Script marked for mix

When you mix your program, don't forget your viewer. He is probably not going to listen to the sound track on big beautiful speakers like those you're mixing to. Most studios can route your mix through a cheaper, smaller speaker, similar to those in movie projectors and television sets. This is where you should judge the mix. Some people prefer to mix the entire program listening only to the small speaker; others mix to expensive speakers, so they can better hear what they're doing, then check the legibility and effectiveness of the mix on a small speaker. Whichever you do, don't forget to listen to the mix as your viewer will; his reaction is the only reason for your program.

Montages

A montage is a series of related shots, changing from one to the next with little or no continuity. They're normally cut faster than normal. Frequently they use computerized visual effects, in addition to the traditional dissolves and wipes. The message of a montage is not in any one individual shot, but in the combined impact of the whole. Often montages are used to communicate feelings, or moods, rather than specific information.

Most television commercials are montages, as are many music videos. Montages are used frequently under opening and closing credits on TV programs. They make effective recaps at the ends of programs to remind the viewer what's he's seen and heard.

Want to quickly establish a Las Vegas location? Show a montage of casino signs and roulette wheels.

Want to impress on the viewer how many different kinds of flowers grow in Texas? Show him a montage of Texas flowers.

Want to show that a character is depressed? Show a montage of shots of him sleeping late, overeating, not washing, walking alone on dreary days.

If any form of film or television can be called art, it's probably the montage. As such, it obeys no rules. Most effective montages, do, however have one thing in common: they all follow the Great Underlying Rule of Editing--each shot is clearly different in content, framing, or both, from the shot before. If the shots were not clearly different, they would blend together and lose their impact. Many good montages also have some sort of progression: they tell a story, or they go from big to little, early to late, pastel to full color, New York to Los Angeles, wide shots to close ups, solo instruments to symphony, etc.

If you are shooting specifically for a montage, I recommend storyboarding it first; make simple drawings of all your shots so you can see how they'll fit together. If you're working from existing material, do a paper edit, just as you would for an unscripted program.

Cutting montages to music.

Montages are often cut to match a piece of music. Music can reinforce the message of the montage.

There's a right way and a wrong way to cut a montage to music. The wrong way is to find a piece of music, start cutting in shots at the head, and keep going till you get to the end. Unless you're very talented or very lucky, this method will not yield the best results. More than likely, you'll find yourself

fifteen seconds from the end of the music with only one not-so-
great shot left to cut in. It's better to work from a plan.

First, make a visual cue strip, showing exactly where you
want to make your cuts to match the music. If you're working on
film, run a piece of clear leader in sync with the music; as the
leader goes through the editing machine, use a black grease
pencil to tap out the musical rhythm directly on the film. Play
back the music and the marked leader, erasing and adjusting your
marks till they hit exactly where you want to make your cuts.

If you're working with video, lay down your music with black
picture, color bars, or any other consistent visual. Now cue up
a long take of a different visual on your play machine. Start a
video-only insert edit with no end point indicated. As the edit
is executed, tap your finger on the insert record button, turning
it on and off to the rhythm of the music. This will give you
alternating scenes representing the cuts in your montage. Repeat
the operation till you're satisfied.

Once you have your visual cue strip, either on video or film,
make a list of the cues, indicating with simple drawings or words
what the music is doing at that point. For example:

1. 2 sec 15 fr   drum roll builds

2. 10 fr   drum boom

3. 10 fr   drum boom

4. 5 secs   horn (peak at 2:05)

Etcetera

Now, make a list of the shots you have available for the montage. Compare the two lists. As you decide where you're going to put each shot, write it in on the music cues list. When the list is filled in, start editing. On film, assemble the montage in a synchronizer with the marked clear leader as a guide. On video, blanket the visual cue scenes with your selected shots.

This method avoids the majority of cutting and splicing and resplicing tiny pieces of film--or dubbing and redubbing on video--as you experiment and change your mind. You'll probably still make some changes, but many fewer than if you worked without a plan.

Divorce the editor.

Just as the director going into editing must divorce himself from everything except what works in the editing, so the editor must divorce himself from his work in order to judge it properly.

The ideal is to put the edited program on the shelf, walk away, and come back a month later to look at it. You usually can't do that. The alternative is to try to blank your mind and look at the program as if you never saw it before. Judge everything by one standard--does it deliver my message to the viewer? Will the viewer react to this the way I want him to? Throw out or change anything that doesn't meet the standard.

If possible, show the program to viewers similar to your target viewer. Listen to their opinions. Don't be quick to discard any suggestion; even the stupidest remark can tell you something about how your program is working.

Final Advice

One of the basic principles of communication is this: to get information across, repeat it. If you glance back through this book, you'll find that I've repeated, in a number of different ways, three basic ideas.

First, film and video production is a craft with rules which can be mastered.

Secondly, the purpose of any program is to get the viewer to react the way you want him to.

Thirdly, the way to get the viewer to react the way you want him to is to tailor the content and style of your program to the viewer.

I've discussed a number of rules. While it's true that many talented film and video makers routinely break the rules, they also routinely get terrific results. Unless you're confident of equal success, I suggest you first work according to the rules.

Still, whenever you have the time and the money, please do try new and different things; it will help you to grow and become better at your craft.

It's okay to fail, as long as you learn from your failures. Don't waste time gloating over your successes; learn from them, too. Professionalism consists of repeating your successes and not repeating your failures.

Start thinking about your program as soon as possible. Let your ideas incubate in your brain; your subconscious will work for you.

Spend as much time planning as possible. Clearly define your goals and how you can reach them. Beware of hidden goals, like winning a prize, showing off your fancy camerawork and editing, or seeing how much money you can save on the budget. The only goal you should have is your viewer's reaction.

If you're ever in doubt about what to do, remember your viewer. Make your program for him. Make him react the way you want him to. Remember, nothing exists except what you show him. All that matters is what's on the screen.

If you have ideas to make this book better, please write

Tom Schroeppel

3205 Price Avenue

Tampa, FLorida 33611

Index

About the Author

Tom Schroeppel is a writer, director, cameraman, and editor living in Tampa, Florida. He has been working in film and tape for more than twenty years. His credits include documentaries, industrials and TV commercials throughout the United States and abroad. He has worked as a training consultant at television stations in Latin America and the Caribbean.

**THE
BARE BONES
CAMERA
COURSE FOR
FILM AND
VIDEO**

**BY
TOM SCHROEPPEL**

Also by Tom Schroeppel, author of
VIDEO GOALS: GETTING RESULTS WITH
PICTURES AND SOUND,

**THE BARE BONES CAMERA COURSE FOR
FILM AND VIDEO**

"THE BARE BONES CAMERA COURSE...is, truly, I'll say it again and again, a marvel of clarity and conciseness."
> Nestor Almendros
> Academy Award Winning Cinematographer
> "Days of Heaven," "Kramer vs. Kramer"

"Schroeppel's...years of experience in editing, directing, and camera work are evident in lucid explanations of function and technique, accompanied by simple but effective graphics that demonstrate classic visual literacy."
> BOOKLIST
> American Library Association

Partial contents: How the camera works, Exposure, Color temperature, Using light meters, Lenses - wide angle, normal and telephoto, Zoom lenses, Focus, Depth of field, Composition, Rule of thirds, Leading lines, Camera angles, Screen direction, How to cross the line, Using screen direction to solve shooting problems, Making camera moves, Lighting, Using reflectors and bounce lights, Planning and shooting a sequence, Storyboards, Shooting out of sequence, and more. Over 200 illustrations. 89 pages, 8 1/2 x 11.

TO: Tom Schroeppel
    3205 Price Avenue
    Tampa, FL 33611

Please send me _____ copies of *The Bare Bones Camera Course for Film and Video* at $8.95 each, plus $2 postage/handling per book.

I enclose check or money order for _____ total.

Name (Please print)_____

Address_____

City _____ State _____ ZIP _____

Florida residents please add 6% state sales tax

Teachers: write on your letterhead for special volume discounts.

TO: Tom Schroeppel
    3205 Price Avenue
    Tampa, FL 33611

Please send me _____ copies of *Video Goals: Getting Results With Pictures and Sound* at $9.95 each, plus $2 postage/handling per book.

I enclose check or money order for _____ total.

Name (Please print)_____

Address_____

City _____ State _____ ZIP _____

Florida residents please add 6% state sales tax

TO: Tom Schroeppel
    3205 Price Avenue
    Tampa, FL 33611

Please send me _____ copies of *Video Goals: Getting Results With Pictures and Sound* at $9.95 each, plus $2 postage/handling per book.

I enclose check or money order for _____ total.

Name (Please print)_____

Address_____

City _____ State _____ ZIP _____

Florida residents please add 6% state sales tax

TO: Tom Schroeppel
    3205 Price Avenue
    Tampa, FL 33611

Please send me _____ copies of *Video Goals: Getting Results With Pictures and Sound* at $9.95 each, plus $2 postage/handling per book.

I enclose check or money order for _____ total.

Name (Please print)_____

Address_____

City _____ State _____ ZIP _____

Florida residents please add 6% state sales tax

Teachers: write on your letterhead for special volume discounts.

COMMENTS ON *VIDEO GOALS:GETTING RESULTS WITH PICTURES AND SOUND*

"Overall, a very valuable guide to the pragmatic elements of the film and television production process. The text is clear, honest and helpful, not pedantic."

> Jay B. Korinek
> Professor, Mass Communication
> Henry Ford Community College
> Dearborn, Michigan

"Your practical experience makes you an especially valuable source of information for production-oriented students."

> Patrick McLaughlin
> Visiting Instructor
> School of Communication
> Grand Valley State College
> Allendale, MI 49401

"I found your book to be well thought out, carefully planned and executed smoothly...you did a terrific job organizing a lot of helpful information into a well-produced textbook."

> Ray DeTournay
> President/Executive Producer
> DeTournay Productions
> Los Angeles, California

"You've taken the 'mystery' out of video production and made it a practical and logical process. My students enjoy reading your book...and they don't enjoy reading."

> Ann E. Eskridge
> Instructor, Mass Media Program
> Golightly Vocational Technical
>   Center
> Detroit, Michigan

"*VIDEO GOALS* is the kind of book everyone should read or reread before a directing or editing session--it can help anyone do a better and more professional job."

> Sandy Mielke
> Independent Producer/Director
> Miami, Florida

ISBN 0-9603718-2-6

90000>

EAN

9 780960 371822